MASS

Essays on Memory, Language, & the State of Massachusetts

Buick Audra

Published by Trimming The Shield Records
Braidwood Drive
Nashville, TN 37214
www.trimmingtheshield.com
www.buickaudra.com

ISBN: 979-8-218-26749-0

Cover design by Buick Audra

"Mass." *Webster's New Collegiate Dictionary,*
a Merriam-Webster. 1980.

For twenty-seven.

Contents

Foreword

In the summer of 2015, I had a friendship end. It was surprising and swift, and it sent me reeling. I had set a simple and clear boundary with a woman when she compared something of great importance to me to a cult. The sentence I texted to her was, "I don't think I'm the right person for that comparison." And that was it. Five-plus years of intimate (or so I thought) friendship, over. It took a few final, dying gasps in the weeks to come, but we never really spoke again, not as friends anyway. Pronounced dead on July 3rd, shortly before a large branch would fall from my neighbor's tree onto my fence. Flattened.

The grief that came up was familiar, but there was something else beneath it. Something worse. It wasn't just that I had lost a friend. It was that I secretly feared that I was incapable of ever holding on to one, especially a woman. I started jotting down names. Over the coming days and weeks, a list emerged. All women. The Lost Women, as I would come to call them. And at the top of that list was a name I hadn't said aloud in years. Behind her, was an entire landscape I'd been avoiding.

Boston.

My mother moved us from Miami to the Boston area when I was nine. It was her move away from my brother's father and all that their handful of years together had held. We had lived in Massachusetts before as a family, but only for short bursts. We always ended up back in Miami. But this move, the one that she made without a partner, this move was definitive. And so would begin my life of forever being from out of town. It continues to this day.

My mother would kick me out four years later and I would end up in Miami for two and a half years, but then it was back to Boston after that. I graduated from high school there, I attended college there, and in a way, I became a little bit from there. But only a little bit. Many things did not stick. The language, the myriad dialects and their colloquialisms, and the cultural markings: none of it took. But I could draw you a map of Harvard Square from memory right now if necessary. Let me know if you ever have a need for such a thing.

The long and short of it is, I am not from Massachusetts, but I'm not *not* from Massachusetts. Regardless (or irregardless, as some folks from Mass are fond of saying), it left its marks on me. I did not look at those marks for more than a decade after leaving. It had been bad. No wonder I hadn't wanted to bother.

But I'm bothering now.

This autopsy has been performed in sections, through various methodologies. The first, was a comprehensive look at the Lost Women with a trusted confidante and mentor. This process took two and a half years and employed Al-Anon's 12 Steps. The second, was during the writing, recording, and release of my third full-length solo album and corresponding memoir in essays, *Conversations with My Other Voice*. Creating that work about my relationship with my voice allowed me to explore what had happened in past chapters within the safe structure of an album format, and within the confines of the companion essays. But I knew there was more. More for later. To be continued, I thought.

And then Marc died. In late June of 2020, I received an email from a longtime friend, someone from the Boston days. He wanted to let me know that my old friend Marc Orleans had died; he wasn't sure if I'd heard yet. I hadn't.

Suicide, he said. A word that still hovers around my memories of Marc as an abstract, shapeless thing I can't ever get my head around. And underneath my shock and sorrow lived something else. A new awareness. That awareness made me sit with what existed of the Boston memories, which were sparse until they weren't.

Once I could see the literal and figurative lay of the land, I started to hear the music. When it had all shown itself, Jerry and I drove up to that mythological land and recorded the work there.

This body of work is the companion writing to the album, *MASS*, by my band Friendship Commanders. It was recorded in Salem, MA, by Kurt Ballou at his GodCity Studio. The essays and album are both intended to be consumed in order, together if possible.

The things I do not own are not on these pages; the things I do, are here.

I did my best. I hope it finds you wherever you are.

Buick Audra

I.

If you don't yet have the language for what you want to say, you will.

Definitions of *mass*

1 (n)

1 : the liturgy of the Eucharist esp. in accordance with the traditional Latin rite

2 : a celebration of the Eucharist

3 : musical setting for the ordinary of the Mass

2 (*n*)

1a : a quantity or aggregate of matter usu. of considerable size

1b : (1) expanse, bulk

(2) massive quality or effect

(3) the principal part or main body

(4) aggregate whole

1c : the property of a body that is a measure of its inertia, that is commonly taken as a measure of the amount of material it contains and causes it to have weight in a gravitational field, and that along with length and time constitutes one of the fundamental quantities on which all physical measurements are based

2 : a large quantity, amount, or number

3a : a large body of persons in a compact group :
a body of persons regarded as an aggregate
3b : the body of people as contrasted with the
elite—often used in pl.

3 (*v*)

(*vi*) to assemble in a mass
(*vt*) to form or collect into a mass

4 (*adj*)

1a : of or relating to the mass of the people;
also : being one or at one with the mass
1b : participated in by or affecting a large number
of individuals
1c : having a large-scale character

5 (*abbr*)

Massachusetts

I ran out of Boston like it was on fire. Like it was a burning building I had to evacuate, leaving everything I had ever owned behind to smolder. Once I was gone, I regarded the place like it had actually burned to the ground, and like the city that still existed was a sort of prop town, a replica. I visited my loved ones there, but I had moved on, started anew. It would be years before I would sort through the rubble and admit what I had lost there.

When I started to assess the damage, I mentioned the awareness to my brother. From Massachusetts soil, he replied, "You had a good life here."

He wasn't wrong. He also wasn't right.

Blue

February 10, 2017, 8:15 PM Central Time

Is this Buick who lived in Belmont? I will never forget . . . kids were making fun of me because I was wearing the same outfit every day and you stood up for me big time! You were the first person I looked up to. You are special to me. I see that you are still making a difference in this world, and I am proud to have known you first and have had you defend me like you do everything that you believe in.

* * *

I had wondered about her for most of my life. We hadn't seen each other since the middle of our eighth-grade year, during which we both disappeared. She stopped showing up at school and I got kicked out. Neither of us knew what happened to the other. As for the bit about standing up for her, I didn't

remember it. But I have a thing about bullies, always have.

I recently saw an article that said people who were bullies as kids don't remember their actions into adulthood. It begs the question: what about people who were bullies as adults? What do they remember?

* * *

I travel back to Boston about once a year on tour, sometimes twice. I prepare myself for days in advance. I make a list of what I know to be true of myself today; I keep it close. I take note of which people I can call if I find myself in a state of panic. Once I'm there, I make no social plans, I don't stay with family, and I don't tool around town visiting where I used to live or hang out. I drive to the venue, I eat nearby, I play, and I leave the next morning. I smile and hug the people I know; I do my level best to perform under what are—for me—extreme emotional conditions. I engage in light conversation with whoever shows up, but ultimately: I'm on a clock. I'm surviving, and there's only so long you can be in that mode without doing serious damage to yourself.

For years, I didn't ask myself why any of this was true, why Boston was so difficult for me. I just accepted that it was and planned accordingly. I also couldn't remember some of it. People would message me from time to time and talk about things we'd done together or things I'd said, and while the stories sounded like me, I couldn't recall much of it. I forgot entire people altogether. To be clear, I am a person who can still remember my first real boyfriend's mother's birthday (February 28th). I can remember what I wore to my first ever concert (Blondie) at age five—and it's not because there are photos; there aren't. I know all the words to songs I hate. My mind holds onto things, including some I wish it didn't. But much of Boston had either been erased or put somewhere dark. I did a lot of nodding and agreeing when people invited me to reminisce; I learned that light laughter can make you look like you're on the same page. But if I'm honest, I didn't know what any of them were talking about. I never got the page number, and I couldn't see the page.

My band's former booking agent, an affable man who lives in Boston but is from elsewhere, once said to me, "Someone said you used to live here, said they used to know you." Friendship Commanders were mid-load-in on a very hot day in Allston, having just arrived to play a small festival that our agent was co-producing. I said, "I did, for kind of a long time. But I have a hard time coming back here." To his credit, he appeared to understand. I'm not even sure that I did. Luckily, there were amps to haul and merch to set up. Tasks are good when you're barely getting through it. They give you something to do. I would be long gone in eighteen hours; I could worry about the "why" of it all later. Some people never do, and that was almost true of me.

* * *

I have always remembered this part.

I was moved back to the Boston area for the third and final time when I was sixteen. I had spent the previous two-and-a-half years in my hometown of Miami, on a punitive sabbatical from my Northern life. My mother kicked me out and sent me to live with my younger brother's father in the middle of my eighth-grade year. She later followed me to Miami herself, and even later, decided my brother and I needed to move back North with her. I spent my first summer back in New England in the home of my best friend Jared's father, a psychotherapist named Arthur. Arthur had known me nearly half my life at that point and treated me like I was an obvious extension of his household where his two sons spent half their time. Their mother lived less than a mile away. The boys spent the rest of their time with her. I didn't go over there if I could help it. She saw me as some sort of threat, in the special way that mothers of boys sometimes see girls. But I wasn't a threat. I was a kid.

Jared and I had been friends since elementary school. Our mother's houses were two streets apart at the time, my house being directly across from the town's public middle school. My brother Bo and I were part of a small group of kids who built and skated plywood ramps in the school's parking lot. Bo and I had matching bright pink Tony Hawk decks. Jared, his younger brother, and a couple of other guys were our crew. I was the only girl, but we were young enough not to know exactly what that meant. Jared and I ended up being closer to each other than we were to the others, and he was a loyal friend to the bone. When I was sent to Miami, he called me every day for the first few months. We wrote letters. We spent our summers dyeing our hair and ruining his mother's towels. Upon returning to Belmont before my eleventh-grade year, he was the only friend I'd known steadily through the Miami years.

That first summer back, I slept on a twin mattress on Arthur's living room floor at night and ran around Harvard Square during the day. My mother and brother wouldn't return to the area until the end of the season. I had left ahead of them, unable to imagine spending even one more day in Miami. That chapter had held at least one form of rejection from each of my three parental figures, a family-wide reaction to my admission of having been sexually abused in my childhood years, and a casually disastrous first love experience. Boston wasn't any better, per se, but it was familiar; it was fifteen-hundred miles away from all of that; and for two glorious months, it was parent-free. Arthur kept an eye on me, and he even gave me a weekly allowance, but he wasn't my parent. He was something safer. He was an ally.

Returning to the area as a proper teen who could go to shows and do as I pleased breathed new life into me. Getting around Miami as a kid was both dangerous and time-consuming. Boston was a walking town, a bus town, and a T town. Later that year, I also got a bike. My freedom knew no bounds. And in that particular moment, Boston was alive.

Belmont is right next to Cambridge, and Cambridge was full of music venues. One block alone held both stages of the Middle East, as well as T.T. the Bear's Place. Any club-level band or artist who could afford to tour the Northeast came through there. There were also myriad smaller, bar-level venues for local acts. And if you had no money to your name, you could stand on the corner in Harvard Square and watch Mary Lou Lord play her singular brand of folk punk. The first time I ever heard the song "Polaroids," it was performed by Mary Lou. She said it had been written by her friend Shawn Colvin. I would later learn every word and note.

Mary Lou would tell stories about dating Kurt Cobain, about making records with her friends, and then she'd play a song by one of them. Her own compositions were peppered among them, but you had to know what you were listening for to catch them. One night when

Arthur and the kids were out of town and I was staying at the house alone, I met two guys who were also watching her play. One was goth and the other was punk. They came home with me to Arthur's and spent the night there. We made microwave quesadillas and listened to Jane's Addiction all night. The punk wrote his phone number on the dry-erase board in the kitchen the next morning, which happened to be his sixteenth birthday. His name was Levi, but I started calling him Mel later that year, short for Melvin. I still do.

I wasn't old enough to get into most shows, but there were ways around that. Patience paid. If an event was 18+, I'd sit outside the venue on the sidewalk and hope an adult would use their elder status to get me in. It worked more often than you might expect. I was finally able to see some of the independent bands who couldn't make it to Miami for logistical and financial reasons. Boston was a hub. But beyond the steady stream of music that passed through, the local scene was robust. Even more exciting: many of the local rock musicians were women. I'd grown up around several female musicians, my mother among them, but as I moved into my own musical sensibilities in my teens, I was surrounded by dudes. Miami had been one band of guys after the next. But not Boston. Those women were out in full force.

Newbury Comics in the Garage allowed kids with no money and nowhere else to be to mill around and look at the same forty records over and over. There was also a Tower Records a block away, and a bookstore called WordsWorth that made me both a reader and a writer. It was three levels, and on the lower level, they had feminist literature, women's studies, and poetry that I sat on the floor and read for free. I bought books as I could afford to, but I read my weight in free pages by Margaret Atwood and Susan Sontag in those hallowed aisles.

Belmont High would be my fourth school in three years. I was primed to adapt, to drop in wherever I landed. But this time, I wasn't going to be the New Kid; I was going to be the Kid Coming Back. But back from where, exactly? In a town where everyone had grown up together, played soccer since the first grade, and would likely stay in the area after they graduated, you didn't just say that your mother had kicked you out to go live with your brother's father, and that you had outed a pedophile while you were there. No, you didn't say that at all. You dressed it up by saying you'd gone to live with your dad while you studied voice at a performing arts school. That was the camouflage.

I was from things that had to be spun, especially in Belmont. My younger years there had taught me where I fit and where I did not. I was being raised by a single parent, I was from somewhere else, and I didn't care much about sports or god. When we first moved to Belmont when I was nine, all of that practically glowed in the dark. Sometimes you don't know how different you are until you see the way someone else looks at you. I spent a chunk of my first year there being shunned by girls who had previously been friendly. Then, the pall lifted just as suddenly as it had set in, and it was childhood as usual. There was a hardness to those kids that wasn't familiar to me, a tone to their collective energy. I could never quite adopt it, but I would learn to mimic it later on.

Once my junior year started, I identified a few other outsiders, more than had been present in middle school. We had multiplied, and at sixteen, we were willingly visible. I hung with two other girls who were both new to town that year, and my boyfriend who lived in Mattapan but was part of Boston's METCO program. He and a few dozen other kids were bussed into Belmont for school. Jared also went to Belmont High, but we had no shared classes or routes. Our friendship existed after school and on weekends, as it always had.

Tuesday nights, I went out to a narrow house on a residential street in Arlington. It was a recovery house, meaning it hosted an assortment of 12 Step meetings across the three primary programs: Alcoholics Anonymous, Al-Anon, and Alateen. We were in the latter program, and our group ranged in age from eleven to nineteen. There were always two adults present, to oversee and moderate, but we ran the meetings ourselves. For one hour on Tuesday nights, I told the whole truth. No camouflage. Whoever we were outside of that room didn't matter in there; no one was popular or left out, and no one was dominant. We were equals who took each other seriously. We treated it like it was life or death. For some of us, it was. I had been in Alateen since I was nine. It was the easiest, safest hour of every week of my kidhood.

By my senior year, I wanted to leave Belmont High. I was spending all of my time in and around Cambridge, and I'd had enough of being one of the weird kids in Belmont. Plus, I'd had an incident during my junior year that landed me up against a locker being told in no uncertain terms that I was out of my lane. Message received. My mother let me lie to the school system and say I lived with her friend Chloe in Porter Square so I could go to the Cambridge Rindge and Latin School just outside of Harvard Square. Unlike Belmont High, it was a city school with kids from all over the place. I could blend in, finally be one of many. If I couldn't belong anywhere, I might as well go unnoticed.

Mel went to Rindge, as did some of his punk friends. Additionally, I befriended someone whose life was about as different from mine as one could get, but with whom I shared a few struggles and a sense of humor. We spent more time at her house than mine and would often sneak out through her parents' kitchen in the middle of the night and ride our bikes through Belmont and Cambridge. We cracked ourselves up by taking our bikes through the all-night drive-through window at the Dunkin Donuts near Alewife Station. We took the donuts to JFK Park and sang our favorite songs a cappella into the late-night air. I shared my love of "Polaroids" with her, and it was added to our late-night repertoire. It felt like life at its finest, its most pure.

During my senior year, I had three morning classes and worked full-time at the Garment District, a three-level factory building in Kendall Square that had been turned into a used clothing oasis. It held two different business operations: Dollar-a-Pound and the Garment District. The former was exactly what it sounds like. People dug through mounds of clothing and filled bags that were then weighed and priced accordingly. The broke kid's dream. The latter, which was upstairs, was the vintage store to end all vintage stores. It held curated collections by both genre and era. And what's more: almost everyone who worked there was in a band. When I started at seventeen, I was the youngest employee by about seven years. I was in heaven. Not only did I get to be around many of the local musicians whose bands I liked, but I was on their guest lists.

My manager was a soft-spoken woman whose hair was cut exactly like Louise Brooks' and who wore impeccable dresses from the 1930s and 1940s every single day. She was patient and gentle, and I adored her. But outside of that place, she played bass and sang in a band with two guys, and seeing her switch to that role was a revelation. She howled on stage. Her voice came up from somewhere deep, guttural. She didn't seem to care about whether or not it was pretty, or whether it colored within the lines. It was delivered from a more honest place.

She wasn't the only one. There were dozens of women right around me who ripped. They were more compelling than their male peers, though there were often men in the bands. I was watching people make work and present it with no concern for how it might be received, no regard for being likable. The work stood and that was the end of it. It wasn't even clear if those women knew the rest of us were in the room when they played. They were doing it anyway. I couldn't wait to be one of them.

There was one thing that existed as an invisible barrier between me and most of that particular rock scene, though. Substances. I was young, but I was also already sure I would never use substances. I had taken a long look at the people I came from and determined that, at the very least, my genetics wouldn't help me out. Plus, I was afraid. Altered states and what they led to frightened me. And it seemed to me that I was the only person looking out for me, so I'd better stay awake. The rock scene had no such inhibitions. Boston was incredibly altered. The drugs were hard, and the lifestyles followed. I remained ever slightly outside of it. Being substance-free also glowed in the dark, so I nominally aligned myself with the straightedge movement, though I had reservations about the dogmatic, dominantly male tone of that culture, too. I had grown up around hardcore music and its cultures. And what people rarely acknowledged, was the violence. It was willfully and knowingly violent. I had been injured several times at shows. I'd had my clothing ripped off.

What I didn't dare say aloud, was that I was afraid of the substance users because of what they might do unintentionally, and I was afraid of the substance abstainers because of what they might do *intentionally*. I tried to find neutral ground in the grey between. Sometimes identifying who and what you are looks like naming who and what you aren't. Sometimes you can find your way by reverse-engineering what you know so far.

As I inched toward adulthood, I stopped in to see Arthur every few months. His house became a base for me, a place I went to reset my dials. Sometimes he was home, sometimes he wasn't, but I was always welcome to be there. He didn't ask how it was going or pry about what had happened in Miami. He didn't need me to say, "She beat me up," or, "They told me none of it ever happened; they called me a liar." He knew.

He understood that no amount of advice was going to save my life, but gentle consistency and the occasional plate of food might. And it kept me coming back.

There's comfort in a space that holds its shape over time, and in people who ask few questions. The living room remained the same, but they eventually moved the twin mattress out of the middle of the floor. I had slept there that first summer with no doors, no dresser, and no closet. Just a bag, my headphones, and a copy of *Badmotorfinger* that I listened to over and over like it was the only album on earth. It might as well have been.

It was the simplest time of my life.

Fail

June 28, 2020, 4:28 PM Central Time

Hey Bu-

I just found out from Terence that Marc Orleans killed himself recently. I know you were friends, and didn't remember anything bad happening with him (though I may just not be remembering, in which case I apologize), but I thought you'd want to know. Sorry to be the bearer of yet more bad news.

* * *

I looked at Marc's number in my phone to see if it was still there. It was. I could call him and check. Call him and see what his voicemail said. I didn't, but it crossed my mind that I could. Maybe it was a mistake. Maybe he'd answer.

Marc. My pal. My blue-eyed, guitar-playing pal. Nothing bad had happened between us . . . ever, now that I was thinking

about it. How rare. In a story that held so many endings and dark chapters, nothing had gone down with Marc. It had been easy, what we had. And foolishly, I thought it was forever. I was learning that "forever" ended the day one of you died. And Marc was dead.

* * *

My late teen years were largely defined by shows, guys, and jobs that paid too little. High school was over, and with it, many relationships and ways of life. Every person who ever writes a lengthy promise of friendship in your senior yearbook is one more person you can count on never seeing again. We say such wild things when we're young. Wilder still: we think we mean them.

My closest female friend during my last year of high school had disappeared after I asked her a clarifying question about a story she'd been telling for years that didn't quite add up. Our ending was confusing at best, unmooring at worst. We had been intimate comrades, nearly inseparable; our voices had warbled into the late-night air together. One question undid it, and I didn't know what to do with that. "*No bye, no aloha*," as Kim Deal would say. While other female pals had simply gone to college in other states, allowing our friendships to die of natural causes like distance and time, ours had been killed intentionally. It was a first for me.

A close friend from Belmont High had given birth between our junior and senior years and was understandably busy being both an adult and a parent. At the other end of the mortal coil, one of my Cambridge punk scene friends had overdosed and died the summer I graduated. She was nineteen years old. It was a loss that most of us didn't know how to talk about—not with each other, anyway. I had all kinds of vocabulary around addiction, having grown up in Alateen, but having the words doesn't always grant you the space to use them. No one around me in that scene used the word "addiction." The narrative went elsewhere to bad boyfriends and unfortunate accidents. It wasn't my place to say otherwise; it still isn't, I suppose. But in my experience, what we can't name, we can't care for or recover from directly.

Adulthood slammed into place. I decided not to go to college right away, to work instead. I wasn't sure I wanted to study music as much as I wanted to play it, so I waited. Work-life and friends became more primary. The music scene was the backdrop of my whole existence.

One of my jobs was tending to the odds and ends that fell under the banner of Crafts in the basement of Pearl Art & Craft in Central Square. The store itself was huge, but my department was small and populated entirely by women. I was taking some evening classes at Massachusetts College of Art and getting into fabric dyeing and screen printing. Dyes were our department's domain. I might have been working for nearly nothing, but I got an employee discount and first pick of the supplies. It was good enough for nineteen.

As had been true at the Garment District, I worked with a large assortment of musicians at Pearl. I wasn't quite in a band of my own yet, but I was getting there. I started an all-female a cappella choir with Seana Carmody of the Swirlies and Syrup USA. She worked with me in Crafts. We had a rotating cast of other women in music performing with us. It wasn't serious or necessarily good, but it was fun, and it got me on stage, something I both wanted and feared.

I had some other pals in the building, and also some antagonists. The store functioned like a giant middle school complete with cliques, mean kids, and outcasts. Every day was about getting in and out of the building past the cashiers and customer service folks, all of whom were right by the door on the ground floor. That group had whipped up a bizarre adolescent-leaning culture and would fling it right at you while you were trying to live your life. It was best to avoid it.

Marc worked in the smallest, most remote department in the store, Fine Arts. It was the only department on the third floor, the space no one accidentally passed through. You had to be trying to find it to do so. Marc was a painter who had studied in Chicago. He was also a musician I'd been aware of since I moved back. His band Spore had been widely respected and was notable to me because of its guitar-playing female member, Mona Elliott. Mona was one of the women who performed like it was the last night we'd all be alive. By the time Marc and I were working together, Spore was over. But he was playing in an assortment of improvisational projects. He'd gotten away from written music and was deeply committed to the experience of getting on stage and seeing what happened. I couldn't imagine a more frightening and courageous act. He loved it.

He was older than me. Most people were. But our ages didn't come up. Marc and I never had a state-of-the-union conversation where we swapped ages, favorite colors, and core beliefs. We simply started being around each other. As time went on, we did it more often. After a while, we met up every day and ate our lunches together. It was an assumed thing, no discussion required. Later still, we hung out off the clock.

I knew all kinds of guys in the rock scene. There were the overly-sensitive-seeming nice guys. They were the worst. They were the ones who often angled to get physically involved with you, regardless of what else might be in place in either of your lives. There were the guys who had been signed to major labels at one point or another and figured it granted them some level of superiority or access. There were the constant educators who thought all women in music needed to be spoken to as beginners. And then there were the peers. They were a rarer breed for sure.

Marc managed to occupy yet another category: the guy who maybe didn't even notice that I was a woman. We were actual friends. He wasn't waiting for me. He wasn't interested. He didn't have anything to teach or explain. And he didn't brag. He just liked to sit and share an avocado while we talked about other bands or an article one of us had read. To this day, I have had few relationships where the other person pays such acute attention when I speak. He looked right at me and smiled when we hung out. He didn't look away when I looked back at him. He could take it. He could hold the line.

I hope with all that I am that I looked back in the same way.

* * *

I wondered about his instruments when he died. And his shirts. In that order. When I think about Marc, I think about stringed instruments and plaid shirts with snaps. And his glasses. And his hats. There was and is no good way to ask, and no one person.

* * *

I started playing guitar the day same day I started my first band. I knew so little about my instrument on that calendar day, I wrote our first song by writing the guitar and bass melodies vocally and then teaching them to myself and the bassist. That's right. Teach what you don't yet know, folks. Be a pro. I knew melody, though. I had heard music in my head all my life. I figured it would simply be a matter of making those songs come through my hands, so I jumped right in. Sometimes ignoring your own limitations actually works.

Initially, there were four of us. My brother Bo (seventeen), Mel (twenty), our friend John (nineteen), and me (twenty). Bo and I had grown up with John. His family lived in the same little grid of streets that made up the neighborhood we shared with Jared and his brother. We all skated those plywood ramps in that park. When we started the band, Bo had been playing drums for about eighteen months, and a wild cocktail of jazz standards and Gorilla Biscuits songs co-existed in his repertoire. Mel had played upright bass in a high school jazz ensemble and then switched to electric for a couple of indie bands led by big personalities. John played guitar and leaned into the indie/post-punk of it all. And me? I liked post-punk, grunge, and R&B; I'd had a brief stint studying opera and singing in concert choirs, and I knew I belonged in a band. I had gotten ahold of a Fender Mustang (1969 reissue) in Sonic Blue with a red pickguard, and I was ready. Didn't even own a tuner; didn't care. You can only be a spectator in your own sport for so long.

Bo and I lived in a duplex back in Belmont above a woman who probably couldn't believe her great misfortune. He was still in high school, and I was in-between truths. But he was under my charge. Our mother had moved out of state and his father still lived in Miami. I was glad to take him so he wouldn't have to switch schools as we had both done many times in our younger years. We were siblings and roommates, and I signed his school forms. It worked.

Before we moved in together, I briefly lived in an apartment with two women I knew from the music scene. I was the common denominator when we rented our place in Union Square in Somerville. By the end of that nine-month social experiment, they were bonded for life, and I was persona non grata. I was more than happy to live with Bo. Bo was a known quantity and one that I liked.

Because we lived on the second floor and were already in the not-so-good graces of our downstairs neighbor, we practiced in the attic, which we had access to through our apartment. It was a small space with sloping walls that followed the roof's pitch, but we crammed in there and figured out both how music worked and how to be together. It did not occur to me that anything was impossible at that time, and so, it wasn't. We named the band after the house's street address, 33 Slade Simple and true.

John was not long for the project, for reasons beyond his control and curs. We played a handful of shows as a four-piece before he had to move on and take care of himself. And then we were three. My guitar playing up to that point had been angular, built of lead lines that interacted with whatever vocals I came up with. The band's early songwriting had looked like composing sections as a group, playing them about eighty-five thousand times, and then eventually working on the next section. It was less instinctual and more intellectual. I knew about song form and structure, but I was wary of being too loud about it, being what people often call women when we might know something: bossy. Plus, the band's writing process was kind of interesting. I didn't mind the meandering approach at first. And when John was still in the band, we got to play off of each other's parts. When he left, the dynamic changed. I started to write whole songs. It felt like having a superpower.

Bo and I made for easy housemates. We'd grown up together and apart in various households of various adults, but without the presence of said adults, our existence was low-key. He went to high school and worked at a local ice cream shop with a bunch of other teenagers. I worked at Pearl and applied to MassArt to be a full-time student. On the one hand, it seemed like a long shot to try to get into a good school for visual art when I had so little formal background in the discipline. It seemed more fitting for me to study music somewhere. On the other hand, I believed the arts were all dialects of a common language, and that studying one would benefit the others. I took good photos of the work I'd made in the continuing education classes; I wrote an essay about the song "Last Chance Texaco" by Rickie Lee Jones (talk about writing what you know), and I sent it in. You can't lose what you don't have. You can only gain.

I started college at age twenty, the same year I started 33 Slade, the same year I became a guitar player and songwriter, and the same year I played my first show. After years of watching the lives of others and trying to figure out what mine would someday look like, it began. During the season in which I started to make my own work, I stepped into my real self. I finally had something that belonged to me. More than one thing.

Marc would occasionally come out to see 33 Slade play live. He didn't give advice or comment on my gear, two things I've since received from other men in music to an appalling degree. He listened and trusted that I knew what I was doing. In turn, I would watch him on stage and smile at his movements once the music began. He had an internal rhythm that had nothing to do with what we were all hearing in the room. His body rocked front to back, his face turned up toward the ceiling, and his eyes closed like he was listening. To some, it might have appeared as though he was listening to his collaborators on stage. But I always thought he was listening to something inside, to himself. I understood it. I knew about the music within, about how it played whether you let it through or not. We both had it. I liked seeing him use it.

As for me, listening to myself led to more music; studying fiber arts and color photography in art school and combining the two; writing and producing a rock opera about the Boston music scene dynamics, and being braver than I'd previously known myself to be. Once the creativity dam burst, it was all I did. Well, almost all. I also tried to navigate human relationships. That was trickier business, the impulses less clear.

I was surrounded by dudes. I was a woman who admired other women and wanted nothing more than to have them in my life, and I was surrounded by dudes. There was a pervasive retro-feminist narrative that women who weren't positively flanked by other women were suspicious, and not to be trusted. But I couldn't make it last with women, no matter what path the relationships took. Things ended. And every time I heard Harriet Wheeler's angelic voice sing about how she could see how people looked down because she was on the outside, I got it. I got it hard. But getting it doesn't mean you can do a thing about it.

It would be years before I knew that the intimacy I shared with my bandmates, with Marc, with Jared—it was all fine. We were fine. I was fine. I was right where I was supposed to be. And I know that now by how those memories feel in my body. They feel like life. They don't feel like strain, deficit, or death. They don't injure me when I revisit them. They just make me miss the people involved.

Marc left Boston a few years later. He moved to New York, and eventually, I did, too. He got into bluegrass and other kinds of traditional music; eventually, I also made some solo work that dipped into americana. We both loved dobro, but he was the one who learned to play it. We knew each other for many years, and I was never not happy to see him. Not ever.

As the email I received in June of 2020 had quite correctly assessed, nothing bad had ever happened between us by the time he died. That stands out as an absolute miracle. And his number is still in my phone.

High Sun

November 7, 2018, 4:04 PM Eastern Time
So, I'm sure you have no interest in watching
(and I have refrained, out of deference), but
I wanted you to know that I just got this
notification from the YouTube channel
for Billy Ruane's live show archives...

No fucking way.

When I saw the email subject,
I thought it was possibly something
else, but there you were in the thumbnail.

* * *

There I was. Twenty-one. In the static image, I was holding my Fender Mustang, which meant she hadn't yet convinced me to play a guitar that matched hers, but we were already in matching clothing. The head-kerchiefs. My god. My chest vibrated with

41

something familiar as I squinted to look at the thumbnail. I wasn't looking at her; I was looking at me. Looking for evidence of what my body was suddenly remembering. Until that moment, I had (perhaps foolishly) believed that I'd gotten away without a trace beyond my own emotional scars. But here was a video. Horrifying.

"Someone just sent me a video of me and J.," I said to Jerry, who was driving the van. We had played Allston the night before and were blessedly already out of Massachusetts, headed toward the next state.

"What? Why?"

Good question. Maybe I could email whatever entity might be running this posthumous YouTube channel and ask them to take this down. And say what, exactly? "Hi there, this was traumatizing, and I'd really rather not have it exist for other people to see"? That hardly rolled off the tongue. Plus, whoever they were, they were likely in Boston.

And people didn't say shit like that in Boston. Not when I was there, anyway.

I didn't watch it. I'd never watch it, I promised myself. Maybe no one else would, either. Whatever. Sure. Deep down, I believed I had conjured her, like Beetlejuice. Two months prior, I had completed a long and painful inventory of the female friendships I'd lost in my lifetime; I'd finally taken stock of what had happened—and with whom—and I'd made amends. I had looked at my part. At the end, there were three names left. People I would never reach out to again. One of them was there because our ending truly had nothing to do with me, and the other two were there because I was afraid of them: Joss and J. This was J. I had not said her name aloud for several years before doing the inventory. And now, here she was.

I looked at the image one more time. I wanted to hug that kid version of myself in her sad brown sweatshirt, with some assortment of band pins on one side. I couldn't remember that show, but I knew what happened. Inanity. Patty-cake games and weird, unison singing, like we were children.

I started to sweat. *Keep it together.*

I put my phone away and closed my eyes. I had to get my nervous system together. It's hard enough for me to get on stage when there aren't ghosts of nightmares past showing up in my texts. This was nothing. Nothing except proof. *It had happened.*

Earlier that year, Friendship Commanders played a show in Chattanooga, TN. The night was a mess; two of the bands had been thrown on the bill that week. One of them had nothing to do with the rest of us on a musical level. It was a metal and hardcore show, but these women had ukuleles and an act with banter not unlike something from the thrilling days of radio.

Beyond that, they were dressed almost exactly alike. Two grown women in their

thirties, I'd have guessed, in matching costumes that involved leather chaps over very short denim shorts, tank tops, vests, and bandanas tied around their necks. They were acting decades younger than their ages, and everything they did on and off stage was deeply in character, rehearsed. It was off-putting on all kinds of levels, but I was paying attention for another reason. Days later, when they were still on my mind, I said to Jerry, "I have a bad feeling about those two. I have a feeling one of them is being controlled by the other."

Been there.

* * *

It started out innocently enough. A pair of mutual friends introduced us, and we had things in common. Like, she was in a band, I was in a band . . . maybe that was it, but it felt like enough connective tissue at the time. The number of people I've met through other folks who also happen to be in bands is unknowable at this point.

And absolutely none of those relationships warrant any further description or exploration. But this one does. This one made a dent.

I was twenty and she was twenty-seven when we met, an age difference we don't tend to think about later in life, but when one of you is just outside of your teens, it matters. Alas, I was so accustomed to being younger than people in my Boston life. She was also larger than me. She was a tall woman who often wore both heeled shoes and a high ponytail, all of which added up to a big presence. Something in her was drawn to something in me, an alchemy I'm sure I'll never understand. But I was in a particularly available moment of my life, and we became friends.

She was fun, bright, and full of stories. Some of those stories involved people I had long enjoyed the work of, like members of the Washington D.C. hardcore and post-hardcore scenes, the Dischord crew. She had gone to college down there and been a part of that world for a bit. She had done things I hoped to do.

In the first month of our relationship, she brought her guitar over to the 33 Slade house and suggested we write a song together. She had an idea for a verse that involved a dissonant chord that I liked. I suggested a chorus, and before we knew it, we had what I considered to be a starter song; a chalk outline to be filled in later. But not her. She thought it was done. In addition, she wanted us to play the same thing on guitar and sing in unison for the bulk of the song. I knew nothing of this approach. Why would two guitarists play exactly the same thing, much less not harmonize vocally? But I went along. Part of me was curious. A larger part of me was compliant.

There was an immediacy to the relationship. We met, became friends, then collaborators, and then we were connected. This was not unusual for me. I'd been making friends in a similar way for a long time. It was because of the moving. Unlike kids who were born somewhere, grew up there, and knew the same general group of people until they graduated high school, I had been moved around. And even within the moving, there had been moving. I had switched schools nearly every year of my life since pre-school with two exceptions. And two years, I switched schools mid-year. It was a lot. As the new kid, I hoped to be claimed by someone. Anyone. The process of becoming friends was accelerated because of the constant newness. Intimacy was forged in less time because I was always just dropping in. If I was lucky, I got a best friend out of it.

Best friends were badges of acceptance. And I so wanted the badge.

* * *

"Best friend" was present as a term in my life before I even began to form memories. My mother had best friends (Holly, Arnie). My older cousin Erika had best friends (Nina, Laurette). It was something women and girls did, name someone as queen of the lot. High priestess of the friend group. And as a very young kid, that was done for me. The adults decided that my first best friend was a neighbor girl named Stephanie. As I write this, I'm not even sure how I knew her. Did we attend some kind of school together? I doubt that our parents were friends; her father was a surgeon, and my parents were . . . not. The connection eludes me. Nonetheless, we were assigned as best friends to one another and spent some truly unmemorable times together on swing sets and jungle gyms. Then there was moving across state lines and back again, at which point the slate always cleaned itself, like the metallic shavings of an Etch-a-Sketch. New town. New best friend.

I don't mean to say that those girls didn't matter to me; some of them absolutely did. But the verbiage was intense, and not always chosen by us. It was inherited. And even when it was chosen by us, I'm not convinced we understood that "best" left others out. Maybe we did. Maybe that was the point. Maybe I'm calling us all into account.

The first time I remember the term being challenged in my life was when I applied to it to someone who was not a girl. Calling Jared my best friend at age eleven got an unexpected set of reactions from some of the adults. Suddenly, there was the threat of sexuality to be considered, of social correctness, of *how it looked*. Here's how it looked: like two skinny kids passing folded notes and riding cheap skateboards together, happily. We learned the surprisingly difficult way that "best friends" was gender specific. It was sleepovers, it was matching clothing, it was the melding of identities, and it was secrets. *Oh*, it was secrets.

No one tells you to look out for that one.

* * *

I don't remember how or when she started to be known as my best friend, but like a lily that stays closed until it inexplicably opens mid-day on a Tuesday, it happened.

The scene around her was partially informed by her primary band, another duo, and the extended community that came along with her bandmate. He was also her ex-boyfriend. He was in a popular emo band with three dudes. His band with her was less known but had a following just the same. Their music was more sophisticated than the project she and I were doing, but not by much. She only played guitar some of the time in that project, and they both sang, but not usually together. There were songs that were hers and songs that were his. Somehow, he had escaped the unison approach that I was working with. Their general community was elitist, academic, and unfamiliar to me, but it was community.

In the early days, she had strong leanings, interests, and ways about her that were all her own. And I had mine. In my other friendships of the time, that was fine. In ours, it was less so. Sometimes she wanted what was one of ours to become the property of the other, and other times, she wanted to create a new, third thing. Something we were *together*. And because we were in what passed as a band, that became the vehicle. The music was not central. Not in the beginning, and not in the end. The *act* was central. And the act was quite far away from who I was.

First, it was the clothing. It was her idea to dress alike when we performed. This had its limitations right out of the gate. She tended to dress like a subdued member of the B-52's who was on a break from the band. There was an undeniable retro aesthetic to her look, one that I did not share. I was in cords and old t-shirts with Doc Martens. Whatever feminine flair I possessed was limited and non-specific. And it likely involved flannels or hooded sweatshirts. She had a solution for that. We would get matching polyester waitress dresses and wear them with triangle scarves in our hair, sweatshirts optional. Costumes. But costumes as what?

As best friends, that's what. I didn't put that together until more than a decade later, but that was it. Best friends was the brand.

As time went on, I became a garment designer. I had been sewing since I was about nine, first by hand, and later by machine. Because I was already making and printing fabric at MassArt, I wandered over into the world of clothing. I upgraded our look to matching black crepe shift dresses with hand-painted silk chiffon apron panels. We looked cool as hell. But it still didn't make our band any good.

After the wardrobe came the guitars. I had one guitar to my name, the Mustang, and she had two: a Strat and a Univox. This mismatched front would not stand, she decided. She picked out what would become our guitars for the remainder of the time in the band: Kays from the 1960s. They looked great; mine felt like a piece of furniture with a neck.

And last, but certainly not least, there was the movement. I'm sorry to say that there was what can only be loosely defined as a dance. And after that, there was a bit that involved hand-clapping games. When I say that I don't know how I let this happen, I mean it. But happen, it did. And this act of ours performed publicly more frequently than I know or care to remember. I reflect on this with a special kind of awe reserved for one's own past choices.

Mortifying project notwithstanding, it was intense. Not always intense in a negative sense, but intense nonetheless. Nearly every single thing in my life was shared and examined by her. Every like, dislike, habit, tendency, and certainly every outside person: it got looked at. If there was a guy in my life, she interviewed me extensively and then advised. If I had something going on with another woman friend, she judged and offered insight. If I had confusion or grief around anything related to my parental figures, she was right there to offer an alternative perspective. And it was all under the banner of love, of feminism, of friendship. I had been primed for this by every gal pal movie ever made, and every YA book about gangs of girls and women who got into all kinds of hijinks. Meanwhile, there were also films like *Heathers* and *Carrie*, but I'm getting ahead of the story.

* * *

As I rode in the van with my eyes closed and focused on regulating my heartbeat, I realized that something else was true. She would be on socials these days. Of course, she would. Immediate search and block. A cursory search led me to another account, one of a woman who had also been friends with J. back then. I'd known her a little. Not well.

There was a post about J. right at the top of her Instagram. They still knew each other. And she was referring to J. as "The Most Important Person." Oh my god. It was all coming back, washing over me like a fever. I remembered that language. My body remembered more than my mind did.

* * *

I had two lives. I had a Boston life where I lived with my brother, played in 33 Slade, went to college, and had a surprisingly robust social community. I also had a Miami life, where both my biological father and my brother's father still lived, and where I still visited. I was on friendly-but-false grounds with my brother's father, a man I still called "Dad," despite my time living with him in my teens and the fallout that followed. I still occasionally went to see him when I was on break from MassArt. And often, when I was back there, I'd pal around with my first real boyfriend from there, who also lived in Boston and attended Berklee College of Music. We had found our way back to each other as young adults, as friends, and hung out in both cities.

During the Christmas break of my sophomore year at MassArt, I picked him up at his parents' Miami house so we could drive around and feel displaced together, one of our favorite shared pastimes. His family still lived within walking distance of the middle school he and I had attended together for a year and a half. There was another house in that vicinity that had long held our interest. It was the home of my biological father. We had taken to driving by it once per visit, just to see if . . . I don't know exactly. If he was still there. If he was still alive. He had stopped taking my calls when I was fifteen and I hadn't heard from him since. And now we were twenty-one.

It was nighttime. Miami is beautiful during the holiday season, especially at night. People wrap strings of lights around the bases of the palm trees in their yards, and the palms serve as impossibly elegant models. It's still my favorite holiday aesthetic.

We pulled up across the street from the house. There were lights on inside, and the van in the driveway was one we recognized from our teen years. He was still there. He was still alive. From the passenger seat, my friend said, "I dare us to go knock on the door." My scalp tingled. Sometimes I wonder if my hair starts growing when my system is over-stimulated. I didn't say anything for a minute, and then I said, "Okay."

There were glass brick panes on either side of the front door, a very South Florida design. It allows you to see movement and light inside the house, but nothing specific. We stood at the door and paused. We hadn't thought this through. Fuck it, I thought. He was my father. I knocked. Something inside moved. We could see shadows through the glass bricks, but no one came to the door. Horror. But too late, we were already in it. After another minute that felt like a full year of my young life, I knocked again. This time, the door swung open, and my biological father's wife stood before us, angry.

"It's 9 o'clock, Buick," she said. And then she walked away from the door and into another room. The door hung open. *No bye, no aloha.*

My friend and I looked at each other, both of our mouths open. Our eyes were as wide as they've ever been before or since. *What was this? Why was she behaving like that? What, in the living hell, did it matter what time it was?* In all the years we'd known each other, my friend had never met my biological father or his partner. We had been first loves, dated for a year, shared clothing. And he'd never met the man who provided half of my DNA, and now here we were, somehow wildly unwelcome on his front steps.

Perhaps emboldened by my own incredulity, I stepped inside. My friend stayed right with me. It didn't change much, to be two feet closer to the insanity, but we did it. From yet another room, out walked my lanky, nonchalant-to-the-point-of-being-dead-inside biological father. It had been six years since he'd dropped me off in my mother's driveway and said, "I'll call you next week."

Without looking at me, and while still walking toward something else, he said, "You're kinda thin, kid."

Holy shit.

Who were these people? But I would not be flattened. I did what I knew how to do: stay upright, keep talking, and act like I was untouchable. The survivor's way. I explained that I was home from college—oh hey, I was in college! I talked about what I was studying, that I played in a band, that Bo lived with me. He didn't ask me a single question, so I filled in the end of my adolescence and beginning of my adulthood for him. I pretended he wanted to know. He didn't. My friend stood wordlessly beside me, probably unable to wrap his mind around this bizarre non-relationship he was witnessing. His parents loved the hell out of him. This was science fiction.

After fifteen excruciating minutes of me arguing for my own worth as a human being, it seemed like time to leave. In my very best I'm-from-nightmare-people breezy tone, I announced that we had to get going. My biological father nodded. I moved toward him and hugged him. He stood there, his long, thin arms at his side. When I pulled away from that final act of rejection, I looked right at him and said something I did not know lived inside of me.

"I just wanted you to see me in case you don't see me again. See how I turned out."

My friend and I walked back to the van like we were regular people going to a car. Once inside, with the doors closed, we shrieked. For us, for grief, for the what-the-fuck of it all. Something had to be released or we'd explode.

And then we drove to South Beach, took off all our clothes and went swimming. A new baptism. It was over. We'd never drive by the house again. He was dead.

It remains the only time a friend of mine has met my biological father.

When I got back to Boston ten days later, I did what I had been socialized to do. I told my very best friend.

Vampire

August 12, 2021, 3:23 PM Eastern Time

So I stumbled across a curious listing on the Harvard Film Archives site recently, indicating they had a tape of a show of ours. (I think this was the ZBC 25th anniversary thing downstairs at the Middle East.) Below is some more info, and attached is a release they'd like us to sign if we want it to be available. I don't have strong feelings either way, but I think it would be fun for it to be included. What do you think? They can also send us a private link if we want to check it out before signing. I am pretty curious/terrified to see it . . .

* * *

I was less curious to see it. I didn't respond with that truth, but I said I'd think about it. I'm still thinking about it, for the record. Mel and I have always been different about the past, about the band.

I was in the middle of writing my first book, a collection of essays about my relationship with my voice, literal and figurative, and every time I got to the Boston years, it was hard. I knew I had to get into it some in those essays, but to what extent and for how long were moveable pieces. Just enough to get it across. Not enough to suck me in.

Plus, I was starting to process Marc's death in a more comprehensive way, getting closer to what lived beneath the grief. I was remembering Boston. It was tough.

A few months before that email arrived, I attended an online seminar by Dr. Susan Rogers, a recording engineer, producer, author, educator, and Doctor of Music Cognition and Psychoacoustics. She's well known for her work as Prince's staff engineer from 1983 to 1987. Her talk tied the science of hearing music to the emotions we experience as creators and consumers of the medium. I found it informative and helpful. After the fact, I emailed her about something I'd wondered for years. I told her I don't experience music-related nostalgia on the level my peers seem to. I don't have it about music I've made, and I don't have it about music I've loved. I've long wondered if it has something to do with my PTSD. So, I asked her.

First, she said she was so sorry to hear of my traumas. Second, she said no, she didn't think so. She said that it sounded to her as though my relationship with music is akin to a marriage. It's not a hobby or a frivolous thing I play with it; it's my other half, and therefore, it isn't all rosy. She said that she's the same way.

Beyond my lack of nostalgia, there was another thing about the email, about 33 Slade. One of the reasons Mel and I don't have the same feelings about the project is that he left Boston two years before the end of the band. He moved to Seattle. But Bo and I kept going,

and Mel never asked about what happened then. But things happened.

* * *

There were multiple projects, but only one of them belonged to me in any musical or spiritual way. There was the band (are we calling it a band?) with J., and there was another duo that I formed with a guy I'd initially met as a customer at one of my many jobs but had since gotten to know a bit. He was the bass player in a band that had been signed to a few major labels; he was also the primary songwriter in that project. He liked my voice enough to ask me to do a project with him, but not enough to allow any of my songs into the repertoire, or even to write together. He, like J., was older than me, but in his case, by a dozen years. And then there was 33 Slade. I wrote in 33 Slade. I played guitar in 33 Slade. I had agency in 33 Slade. And we were the best project of the bunch.

We graduated from the attic to local stages, to rehearsal spaces, basements, and makeshift studios. We performed in the area a lot. While we didn't make a proper album for the first handful of years that we were a band, we made two sets of demos and played all the time. It was how we hung out as a group. We played. There was always someone letting bands pay rent to practice in some industrial building or another, and we crammed ourselves into all kinds of spaces.

There was the building next to the Edelweiss wholesale bakery location. The floors were so old and unstable, you had to walk on specific planks in the hallways or risk falling through. Once you were in there, you were consumed by the smell of baking bread and confections. There was the building across from the Teddie Peanut Butter factory in Everett. That place was practically baking us. So little air circulated in that space that on hot days, we would all get undressed and play in our underwear, dripping with sweat. Last, there was the building right across Boylston from Fenway Park. That place was legendary. It had a bathroom like the one at

CBGB, and people lived in that building. They weren't supposed to, but they did. You had to make sure not to drive your car there on home game days, but not because of a lack of parking; because your car would be vandalized by unhinged Red Sox fans who resorted to violence whether the Sox won or not.

Ah, Boston.

I loved being in that band, though. I'm not sure I ever said so out loud when we were doing it, but I did. It wasn't our way, or my way, to say so. The band simply was, like my siblinghood with Bo, and our almost-siblinghood with Mel. Those things were givens, and so were our easy musical connections with one another. We didn't talk about it.

My connection with J. was not like that. It did not feel as though we were sisters, but the sameness and togetherness willfully raged on. 33 Slade was the one thing we didn't share. I did occasionally email my lyrics for new songs to her, a habit I'd gotten into with a few of my friends, but it was just to show what I was working on. I was still reeling from the newness of songwriting, that it could tell me what and how I was feeling. It was the way I communicated with myself and everyone else. She received the lyrics and sometimes gave feedback, but only because I didn't know how to say that it wasn't what I was seeking. I was seeking connection, not correction, a distinction that would come later.

There were other things I found difficult to identify and express, even though my body flagged and marked them on the spot. And all of them had to do with identity.

As a person who was given the name Buick at birth, who was born to unmarried musicians, who was shuffled around, who was raised on the music of Miami and its intersecting cultures, and who survived many things in my young years, I didn't feel the same as anyone else. In 12 Step recovery rooms they refer to this feeling as "terminal uniqueness," but I don't think that's exactly accurate. There is an individuality that emerges from such circumstances, and while I had learned how to tamp it down in certain settings as a kid, I couldn't undo it altogether. I felt how I felt. I loved what I loved. I disliked what I disliked. And I have never met another person on earth who has the exact same set of markings.

My brother is the closest in many ways, but even he and I differ in primary areas. For starters, we have different biological fathers. With that, come identities that have been shaped by both DNA and experience. He was wanted; I was not. He has known his parents all of his life; I have not. And then there's gender and all that it informs. The second set of people I feel any kind of kinship with are fellow survivors of abuse, but we differ in myriad ways. What we do with our markings varies widely. Last, I feel a sense of commonality with other adult children of alcoholics, especially the ones who have chosen recovery. But again, we are motley. I am my own person. It can't be undone.

In my friendship with J., especially as I aged into proper adulthood, that individuality became a struggle. Sometimes the struggle was subtle and almost benign. Other times, it was overt. And again, it wasn't just her. It was partially a set of culturally accepted ideas and attitudes. But some of it was her. And I didn't know how to navigate it.

The first flag that went up for me had to do with Prince. Yes, that Prince. The Purple One. I brought my lifelong love of Prince and his work into the relationship, right along with my love of many other R&B, funk, and soul artists. Now, a lot of people love Prince. I'm not claiming any kind of ownership of that. But in our particular dynamic, I was into him. As time went on, that love became her property, and a story developed around the roots of that love. I watched it happen. And at one point, she claimed to be working with him. She once told me that she and a team of other graphic designers were overhauling and redesigning his website. I still don't know if that one was true, but if I loved something, she loved it harder. If I did something, she became an expert at it. If I had something, she found a way to have more of it. And then she told a public story about how it had always been so.

Flag.

The second flag also had to do with honesty. In the seven years I knew her, many things were told to me that seemed potentially untrue. They ranged in scale from this-might-be-an-exaggeration to this-is-an-outright-lie. But there were untruths. And often, those untruths had to do with things relating to me.

Leading up to a 33 Slade show at the Middle East upstairs, J. told me that a hugely influential band had broken up after more than fifteen years of playing together. It was one of my favorite bands, and people she knew personally. I told the dudes, and I ended up writing a song about endings, about choosing to part ways. We got it together for the show, and when we were on stage about to play it, I talked about that particular band breaking up. As we started to play the song, I glanced over at J. and her partner. They were laughing. I felt the world slow way down. I felt my heartbeat in my face.

Laughing.

At me? At what I'd said? Did I make a mistake? I had to focus, keep playing, finish the show. My limbs felt heavy.

Laughing.

After we loaded off stage, J. and her partner walked toward me. Their faces were wide with smiles. I smiled back. But there were questions behind my smile. Without me having to ask, she laughed and said that I had misunderstood, that the band hadn't broken up—but wow, hadn't I taken that a bit seriously? I'd gone and written a whole song about it?

There were two of them and only one of me, but between me and the sky above, she was lying. She had told me *exactly* that the band had broken up. We'd had a whole conversation about it, about the dynamics at play. And now, with this dude and a room full of oblivious show-goers behind her, she was lying to me. And she was inviting me to play along. I didn't do that, but I also didn't announce the truth. I walked toward my bandmates and busied myself with moving the gear to a better part of the room. What a blessed distraction that can be. But I filed it away. She lied and she laughed. The laughing was maybe worse than the lying. I'd seen the lying before. I didn't know what it was about, but I'd seen it. The laughing was new.

Flag.

Last, there were the tantrums. Sometimes the tantrums looked like her sitting in her car for an hour when we were about to play a show, and other times they looked like crying fits in front of other people. I was to blame all around.

Thousands of flags.

Underneath it all, was the management of me. From early on, there was management. The filing down of who I was. I didn't speak to Mel correctly. I sang along with the music too loudly in the grocery store. I ate too many bagels (that one impacted me for longer than I care to admit). I looked too thin when my hair was long. My other friends had this and that issue, and did I really want to be around those kinds of people? It went on and on. And I allowed it. And by allowing it, I chose it.

The tricky part was that it was all done in a way that looked and felt an awful lot like love. We had fun, we laughed, we ran around together, we gossiped. She loved to gossip, and so did I. Part of me knows it's a normal, age-old bonding practice, and part of me knows it can cross a line. Our gossip was mostly about other women. She had a thing about certain women. They liked her boyfriend, or they were some sort of loudmouth obnoxious brand of woman that needed too much attention. (She had a thing about women she thought needed too much attention. Put a pin in that.) And I was invited to—nay, expected to—dislike them right alongside her. The only thing was, I didn't see what she saw. I didn't see toxic, aggressive women who hated the rest of us. I saw Jessica Hopper. I saw Carrie Brownstein. From a distance, they looked alright to me. But I let her be however she needed to be about it.

We talked about other things, too. Our families, our partners, our histories, our fears. Our stories had some parallels, but we were different ways about them. I was hurt by what had happened in my teen years, and what had happened since. She had found a way to look at her absences and presences that made it all okay. Better than okay. *Magical*. She had the right stepfather. Her relationship with her mother was a dream. Her brother was perfect. And the rest? It just didn't need to come up. Simple.

Mine came up. It came up all over the place. And once I started to write music, it went there. 33 Slade had finally decided to make an album. We asked J. Robbins to produce and engineer it, and we booked time at Inner Ear in Arlington, Virginia. It was real. It was happening. It was ours. Mel was already working on moving away from Boston, but we wanted to document the music we'd been making together. Bo and I would continue the project with someone else after Mel left. It was imperfect, but it was what we had. I quit a shitty job to make that record. No regrets.

For the album, I wrote about the death of a guitar player and engineer named Randy Rush. He had been friends with my biological parents before I was born and played in a band with my biological father at some point. When I was a kid, he was always the kindest adult to me, and one of the only ones who seemed to understand that I was, in fact, a child. His death brought up grief around losing him, but also illuminated the profound black spot that my biological father had been in contrast. I wrote about losing Mel to another life chapter so far away. I wrote about interpersonal dynamics that confused me. And I wrote about trying. Trying has always come with costs for me. I have a mother who competes with me. If I win, I also lose.

For many reasons, the record was important to us, to me. I was learning to speak for myself, learning to say what I meant. I had dreamed my whole life of making records and touring. I didn't care about matching costumes and dance routines. I didn't care about duets in Western shirts. I didn't care about making music that made everyone feel okay. I cared about telling the truth. Clothing optional. And we were doing it.

We decided to call the record *The Way to Win: A True Story*. An album about grief, relationships, and daring to try. It was a good idea. And we boldly moved forward with it.

Jump first, recover later. The mantra of my twenties. And sometimes, however unbelievable, it works. If anyone in your life is jealous, remove them.

I only know that last bit now.

Still Life

December 5, 2018, 10:23 AM Central Time
Did you ever record anything with Andy?

Who knows!

Ha! Forgot about deleted files!

Weird, right?
I'm inclined to say no
though, unless with J. and,
I don't think so.

* * *

A guy named Andy had texted and friend-requested me after about two-hundred years, out of the blue. He was coming down to Nashville to work with another engineer here, a dude I know peripherally. Andy, a recording engineer and label person from the Boston days, knew everyone in the world. As it turns out, "everyone in the world" often includes me, whether I like it or not.

The real issue was, he had been close friends with J. back in the day. Quite close.

My eyeballs had a hard time sending the data to my brain at first. Either the world was way too small, or Boston was way too big. Could a person not leave that place completely? Was there always a hand coming up from the grave to grab you? Did you have to move into the witness protection program to break free, or was that run by Bostonians as well?

Christ on the cross, I thought, my grandmother's voice briefly becoming the narrator of my thoughts. I did remember Andy, but not if I had ever recorded with him. If it ever existed, that cognitive file was still missing. I was okay with it.

"Deleted files" was how I made it okay for everyone else.

* * *

"When your hair gets that long, you look too thin, too drawn."

We were working at the dining room table in my brother's father's house in a rural suburb of Miami. We were drafting my wedding dress. I had fallen in love with someone, he had asked, and I had accepted. And now J. and I were in one of the houses I grew up in, sorting out the nuts and bolts of what would become the gown. I had chosen shell pink silk dupioni as the fabric. Strapless. Narrow through the bodice and hip, and then flared. Train. Glass beads. Tone on tone. My first name would be spelled out in the beads across the front of the bodice. Why not? It was true; might as well put it there for all the world to see.

J. couldn't sew. Or design garments. But she had offered to come and help, so we turned it into a whole trip. I knew nothing about how weddings worked. My mother never married, and I was the first of my friends to get engaged. I was making it up on the spot, doing what I wanted. It was fun, it was like putting a production together. Plus, I got to make this dress.

The comment about my hair, which was actually a comment about my body, hung in the air. My hair was long. I had been growing it out. But I was wearing it down, which wasn't typical. I often wore it on top of my head in a big bloom, like her. But I didn't mind it down. I looked across at her. Her hair was up. I didn't have the energy for a discussion. I pulled my hair back and kept moving. The trip was going well, surprisingly. We were actually enjoying ourselves, and each other.

It was a big deal for me to bring anyone to that house, which was called the Brown House in my extended family. Kids had come over when I was living there, but a lot had happened since then. I had been disowned by members of my brother's family since then. I had only ever brought one female friend down from Boston when we were in high school; Mel had come once when we were nineteen; and my fiancée had been there a couple of times. But he was different. We were getting married. For the others, it was momentous. I didn't show this part of my story to people anymore.

But here we were. I could let the hair thing slide.

The vibe with my brother's father was all over the place, but that was typical. We had never quite found our footing after I moved back to Boston. We had no tool set for discussing what had happened, so we just let time pass. Sometimes I tried to pull a Boston and pretend everything was great; other times, I couldn't do it. He was even less consistent than that. As it turns out, there's no easy way to recover from telling someone their father is a pedophile, nor that you remember every single thing that happened in your childhood. Every single thing they hoped you'd forget. No, the handbook on that hasn't yet been published.

Still, he let us have the run of the house while we were in town. He stayed at his girlfriend's place in South Miami, more than thirty minutes away. We only saw him here and there.

Pieces of the dress were laid out in front of us, some in muslin, some in pink silk. We were leaning over them when the gate at the end of the driveway opened. We weren't expecting anyone, so we turned and watched.

The gate sat at the end of a palm-lined driveway. It was two-hundred feet from the front door of the house, a Craftsman-style structure from the 1930s. On either side of the automated wooden gate was a wall made out of sea coral that wrapped around the perimeter of the property. When the gate opened from the outside, it meant someone had a clicker. It was someone the family knew.

The nose of an SUV emerged in slow motion. As the gate revealed more of the vehicle, we saw that it was a Bronco. It wasn't a car I recognized. My body reacted with a swift temperature change and an elevated heart rate. I would later come to recognize these as my trauma markings being activated, but back then, I assumed it was something everyone experienced.

J. was asking questions of a reasonable variety. Her body looked like it had maintained its original settings. I knew I was changing color.

I knew without knowing that it was Hugh, a man I had been raised to call "Uncle Hugh," but whom I called nothing at all if I could help it. I had been afraid of Hugh all my life. And since leaving Miami at the age of sixteen, I'd done my level best to avoid him. But here he was, in person. And I knew why.

The lists of people who might get an invitation to my upcoming wedding were being made. My husband-to-be came from a huge Irish-Polish Catholic family, so the majority of the lists were people he was related to. But I had lists, too. I had given my mother and my brother's father (no longer a couple) the leeway to invite some of their friends if they wanted. My mother's list had been fine. My brother's father's list had included Hugh. For the first time in my life on earth, I had said No to him. It was a hard No, too, not a soft No with room for discussion. It was a No.

My brother's father wasn't used to hearing No—certainly not from me—and he balked. We went a few rounds of him raging and me maintaining my position before I reminded him of a story I'd been telling since I was a kid. The events had taken place when I was five years old, but I could still see them clearly. I had spoken up about them right after they happened, and my brother's father told me they simply hadn't happened. It had come up several times over the years, and his response was always the same: I imagined it.

The story was this: Hugh tried to push me out of a moving car in Martha's Vineyard.

Earlier in the night, his girlfriend and another family friend had taken me into town drinking with them. When they lost their keys at the end of the evening, they called Hugh to come and pick us up. On the drive home, they put me in the front seat, and they sat in the back. He was angry.

Angry at them, angry that his night had been interrupted, and angry that they were giving him shit for being angry. Everyone was in an altered state. They fought with him on the drive home, and his response was to reach over, open my door, and try to push me out while still driving. I told the adults about it the next day, and I wasn't believed. And now it was twenty-one years later.

In the process of standing my ground about the wedding invitations, I had put one condition on the Hugh thing, assuming it would never come to pass. I had said, "If he wants to come to my wedding, he can make amends to me for what he did." And now here he was. No heads up. No call from my brother's father. He had just sent him over to the house.

There was a fleeting moment when we considered hiding. The fear was so great, I didn't think I could stand there and face the man. J. wasn't so hot on the idea either. She knew bits and pieces of my family's story and thought the whole thing was insane. It was.

We didn't hide, but only because we knew he'd already seen us. The house is designed in such a way that you can see right through the whole thing from the front windows. He had probably seen us while the gate was opening. Plus, hiding posed other questions: how long do you hide? Also, where?

We watched him get out of his car and let himself into the house. (This was the other thing about hiding: there were no locks on any of the doors in the house. If you could get through the gate, you were in. It terrified me as a child. I wasn't so wild about it as an adult, either.)

Weak, unenthusiastic greetings ensued. J., being from the outside world, did her best to model normal human behaviors. We did our best to mirror them. He asked to speak to me alone. I agreed. He walked outside ahead of me. I hung back and told J. that if I wasn't back inside in twenty minutes, to call the police. She nodded. We looked into each other's eyes and shared three hours' worth of talking in two seconds.

When I went out back, Hugh was sitting on the far edge of the deck. I stood nearby. My days of sitting were over. I would never sit again.

He looked meek. He said, "Your dad said I had to come and talk to you."

That wasn't *quite* what I'd said, but okay.

I told him I wasn't comfortable with him attending the wedding, the history being what it was.

He looked down. And then he looked up at me, squinting because the sun was in his eyes. He said, "What did I do to you? Did I molest you?"

Oh, holy *shit*.

The man had lost so much information that he wondered if he had sexually abused me.

I told him the truth. I told him everything I remembered. The rage, the screaming, the swinging at Lucy and Bonnie, the trying to push me out of the moving car. I told him that it had traumatized me, that it would never leave my body or my mind—and that after that, he had been an insufferable bully toward me all of my young life. That he had spent most of my childhood naked, that he had been crass and cruel toward me.

He nodded. It looked as though some of that rang distant bells for him. Surely, he knew he hadn't been a kind or loving man, even if he couldn't remember trying to kill me twenty years earlier. I mean, we do know *something* of ourselves, don't we?

Finally, he said, "I'm sorry. I'm sure it happened. And I'm sorry for it."

I had been raised to say things like, "It's okay" when someone did something hurtful to me. But it wasn't okay. So, I simply said, "Thanks." It was the best I could do.

He left, and I told J. all about it. We went back to looking at pieces of muslin and silk. And I knew I would never be normal. I would never have a normal story. But I could make a killer dress and have one goddamned week in Miami. I could and I would. And I would choose to trust this person who had witnessed the second half of one of the most formative and intense stories of my young life.

We went to the mall; we laughed and sang and danced; we drove to Miami Beach. It was one of the best weeks of our friendship.

J. was the maid of honor at my wedding. One of two. I asked another close friend to share the title, and that was a whole thing. I also had three other bridesmaids, and Mel was my bridesdude. I leaned into the wedding thing to a surprising degree. It was a beautiful event. It had its moments, like my mother saying, "Oh, my poor daughter" in the receiving line, and J. wearing a hairpiece that made her about a foot taller than me, but it was a good day. I suddenly had more family, more community, more love. The dress was lovely. People thought the name on the front was funny, and I leaned into that, too. I made jokes about wanting to remember who I was, but deep down, I thought it was cool. Why make your own dress if it isn't going to be unmistakably yours?

My brother's father gave me away. Hugh came to the wedding. He and his partner gave me a vegetable steamer. I still have it.

I did not invite my biological father, but his sister and mother came. I hadn't seen them since he cut ties with me when I was fifteen. He had told them I didn't want relationships with them. That was how he explained my absence all those years. He put it on me, the kid. I didn't know that until I was well into adulthood, at which point I took small steps to know the people I was from in more ways than one.

My brother's jazz ensemble played at the reception; they were fantastic. My old friend Jared DJ'd after that. The tables were sprinkled with guitar picks that had been printed with a photo of me and my new husband, both of us being guitar players. I had pulled it off. In my husband's absence, while he was on tour, I had successfully pulled together a wedding with one hundred and sixty attendees, ninety of which were his family members. We danced all night, and an enjoyable time was had by all, to the best of my knowledge.

I wore my hair up, probably because it was my idea, but maybe because it wasn't. I'll never really know. But I got married in September, and by March, I didn't know J. anymore. On my wedding day, we were in the home stretch. And the glass beads that said "Buick" sparkled in the light, like a beacon back to my own self. *Remember who you are. Hold on to yourself.*

I would need it.

II.

If you're living in a chapter you don't know how to leave, you will.

We Were Here

September 28, 2016, 2:05 PM Central Time

Dear Buick,

I heard the Sundays on the radio and it prompted me to Google you. Thank you for your music--I love Brother Blue in particular. Thank you also for being an unparalleled soulmate and fellow traveler during a rough time, and for my oxblood steeltoe Docs. Hope to know you again.

* * *

Tolerance and patience. Those were the two things I was focusing on in the inventory of lost female friendships that week. I had shared my findings with a trusted confidant two days prior. A list of the relationships where I felt I had practiced tolerance and patience, and a list where I hadn't. She was on the first list. But the friendship had ended

anyway, in a mysterious and immediate way, years earlier.

She was the third woman from the list to find and contact me that year. Each relationship had been lapsed for several years. I noticed a pattern in their communications. They talked about who I had been to them, but not who they had been to me. The invitation to know them again came with a quiet clause. We weren't going to talk about it. *No bye, no aloha.*

* * *

Shortly after my wedding, 33 Slade released our first album, and I got started on the second. I was writing it alone because Mel was gone and Bo was all over the place. He and I were still the core of the band, but we didn't sit around and write together. I brought stuff to practice and we worked it out. When we played live, we had a rotating cast of bass players who joined us. One of them was my first boyfriend, the one who had moved up from Miami. He was a guitarist, but he didn't mind playing bass with us.

In that same season, J.'s partner asked 33 Slade to do a tour opening for his band. They were gaining popularity. It was a good opportunity for us. It was potentially not great for my friendship with J., but I said yes anyway.

Almost immediately after we agreed to do the tour, the frost began. I started to feel a more pronounced version of something I was already quite familiar with. Absence combined with look-at-the-awesome-friendship-I'm-having-with-SOMEONE-ELSE. Someone better. The best, actually. *The best.*

The thing about being the highest is that there's nowhere to go but down.

I got demoted. Whether it was because I was touring with her boyfriend or what, I can't say, even from here. It's not my place to fill in that blank. But the timeline reveals that possibility. In the past when I got the frost for other choices she didn't approve of, I did what was expected of me.

I called. I asked. I made the first move to work it out. For some reason, on the occasion of this early snow, I didn't. I stayed put. I let her be gone. I tended to my own business.

Some of that business involved getting ready for the tour. My Miami friend was set to do the run, the three of us started rehearsals, and we had posters made to send to the venues and hang around Boston. One of the shows on the tour was in town at the Middle East downstairs. I had an idea for a poster. The dudes were down. We arranged a shoot.

The band had gotten some write-ups over the years, and it was not uncommon for those reviews to mention not only that I was female, but also what I looked like physically. Male reviewers would actually comment on my body in reviews as if it had a single thing to do with the music. And never once—not ever—did they handle the guys in the same way. No review described my brother's body type, and his gender was the default. So, I decided to flip the script.

For the posters, we'd all just stand there in our underwear, topless. If they wanted to focus on bodies, we'd give them bodies. Simple, bold, fuck it.

Dagan Barrett agreed to take the photos, I made a giant black fabric backdrop, and in January of that year, we all stood in the dining room of my Dorchester apartment in our underwear. The shots were great. We picked one and that was it. Printed, mailed, hung.

Almost immediately, there was a reaction. The first thing we noticed was that the ones we hung around town were taken down right away. We hung one by the front door of our rehearsal space building, went and rehearsed, and then came out and the poster was gone. I panicked and thought people were ripping them down and throwing them away. We later learned that people were taking them down and keeping them, hanging them in their own rehearsal spaces, on their fridges, etc. The next thing we noticed was the judgment. And it didn't come from where I expected, which was the dudes. It came from other women. They had all kinds of questions. Why? What was I trying to prove? What, exactly, was I trying to communicate?

Fascinating.

This was decades after the Red Hot Chili Peppers had begun their signature brand of stunt nudity, performing with socks on their penises; socks that eventually fell off, rendering the guys completely naked. Decades after Prince and the chaps. Ass out. No one cared at all. And yet, my tits were out, and it required an explanation to my own gender. I did not see that coming, I have to be honest.

The most notable reaction came from J., which was complete silence. I expected that. I might have known it would come. I might have been pushing back against years of being told what to wear, and how. I might have known that being what she considered to be immodest would be punished or worse.

Months passed. The tour rolled around, and we went. Perhaps because of the chasm between J. and myself, perhaps because of something else, there was a palpable distance between our band and the headlining band. With any other group, I'm not sure we would have noticed or cared. But the singer-songwriter at the helm of that project had become like a brother-in-law to me over the years. And now we weren't supposed to go into his green room; now we weren't interacting in any familiar ways. The tour had other issues, not the least of which was my temporary bassist telling me I was tone-deaf every night after we got off stage. But the vibe with the other band was bad, save for two members who did their best to be level, decent dudes.

On the afternoon of our Philadelphia show, we went to a coffee shop to kill time before soundcheck. We leafed through a copy of a local music publication that had been left on a table and stopped when we saw a name we recognized. It was an interview with J. in advance of a festival of female musicians later in the month; she was scheduled to perform. The interviewer asked what was ahead for her, and J.'s response was, "I've actually joined another band. They're called 33 Slade."

It was the first we'd heard of it.

And then we played Boston.

It was a sold-out show. I wore a sheer black shift mini dress with a slight sparkle on the surface. I had made it specifically for the show. Special show, special garment. The room was packed with people we both knew and didn't know. Our topless posters were still taped up in the bathrooms. I got several questions about them that night. I smiled and kept moving. You can do that when you're the one playing. You don't have to defend your every decision on show nights.

The tension with the headliner remained. We moved forward anyway. It was too late. The best we could do was play well, and we did. Matt Squire stood right up front, beaming up at us. He and I were working on the second 33 Slade album together, recording at a studio on the Cambridge-Arlington line called Camp Street. It was owned by Paul Kolderie and Sean Slade, but Squire worked out of it a lot.

I met Squire through my partner, whose side project had recorded a quick-and-dirty punk EP with him. He and I collaborated on some short projects together after that. When I had the body of work that would become the second 33 Slade album, I went to him with it. It was going well.

From the stage, I could see J. toward the back of the room. She was not beaming. She looked like a stone sculpture of herself. There was a stillness to her. It was familiar to me. My mother has that same weather pattern. Like the air between straight-line winds, it can be motionless.

The night was a blur of responsibilities, niceties, and keeping it together. I spoke to J. briefly toward the end of the night. The tone was distant, detached, and professional. Like we had worked together in some office somewhere. Like we had once been sisters-in-law but now had no real connection to one another. Friendly and fake.

We left for the rest of the tour the next day. The shows were packed, we were good on stage, we sold merch, and we pretended it was no big deal that two major things were happening: that the headliner didn't want to socialize with us, and that the interim bass player was trying to convince me I couldn't hear pitch correctly. Every single night, as soon as we got off stage, I had to hear about what I'd sung incorrectly according to him.

Sometimes when there are too many fires raging, you have to pick one and put it out; make one the primary source of heat and discomfort. In that stretch of shows, it was the bass player. I had been dealing with moody, uneven people since I was born. It was nothing new, and it was nothing urgent. But the low-grade erosion of my sense of pitch was another thing entirely. I was having trouble getting on stage with each new show.

We left the tour a day early and didn't play the last show. Sorry, Buffalo. It was a tough time.

I figured I'd be punished by J., but I didn't have the energy to predict what that might look like. After seven years of being corrected by her for far less, I knew I'd face some fallout for both the tour and the poster. I'd risen up and done what I wanted instead of what I'd been trained to do, which was to be small. Be grateful. Be helpful. Instead, I'd taken off all my clothes, sung with my full voice, and acted like myself for the first time in a while. And it had been glorious. I had watched those women tear it up on stage when I first got to town and had finally arrived at that threshold myself. No hand claps, no badly intonating Kay guitar for show, no headkerchief. No leader.

I was the leader. 33 Slade had become my band. I had written the second album on my own and planned to call it *Harmonies for One*. There were a lot of people involved in the album, more than had been on *The Way to Win: A True Story*, but they weren't all band members. Bo and I were the only real members at that point. We had flown Mel back to play on the basic tracks simply because he was the best fit. Initially, the interim bassist had offered to play, but he proved himself to be too controlling. Plus, he wasn't actually a bass player, and in that band, it showed. So, it was the three core members back together on the basics.

Other people had expressed interest in playing on the record, too, including J.; I hadn't said yes, but I also hadn't said no. She didn't really play anything that was needed, and I would not invite that vocal approach into my project. That sameness, that smallness. She didn't love my big voice and I didn't love being reminded of that. I would not allow it in 33 Slade.

For those original sessions, Grant Hart of Hüsker Dü had long been slated to produce. He and I had done months of communicating about the songs and pre-production ideas. Alas, after a couple of short days of working together, the band determined it was best to go it alone. Grant left after the second day and I became the default producer. I shared those duties with Squire, but he deferred to me.

The album was a gift. An intense gift, but a gift just the same. I was telling the truth. I was producing. I was figuring out who I was, one track at a time. Camp Street became a haven for me, its comfort as important as its capacity as a great-sounding room. Paul had a Neve in there, every guitar pedal that had ever been made, an army of guitars, amps for days, and the space was outfitted with cool, mid-century lamps and furniture. I could have lived in there. I had ease in there. And courage.

Bless the rooms that give us courage.

I wrote a song about the seasons of absence I experienced with J., usually in response to something I'd done incorrectly by her standards. The song was called "Shit for Friends," and I wanted it to open the record. In it, I said, "*Some loves are lessons in our own behavior; we figure it out through somebody else*." I was starting to understand my part, that I'd allowed and participated in years of imbalance, of odd power dynamics. I invited a local singer-songwriter named Tess Walker to play piano on it, which was the first time we'd ever had that kind of instrumentation in the project. I thought what she added was thoughtful and lovely.

Another song, "Be the One," had a long ending in which I thought horns might be cool. We asked saxophonist Dave Hess and trumpeter Chris Brown to join us, and they did. The song was me questioning my new marriage and whether or not there was any room for me in it. I had married another musician, and his career was considered primary, more important than mine. And the community around him seemed to see me as an accessory to his life, as opposed to a real living, breathing person. All that to say, the horns were a good call. They added a melancholic, bold texture to the end of the track.

Once everyone else had recorded their parts, Squire and I spent long days and nights getting the vocals and guitar overdubs just right. We found that I sang with more power and abandon in the middle of the night. The vocal for "Shit for Friends" was cut at 2:30 AM and was executed in a single take. I'm proud of that. And I'm grateful to Squire for being a studio rat right alongside me. He seemed to love the process as much as I did. And maybe we were both living through weird moments in Boston at the time. Maybe we were riding out the clock in the sanctuary of a cool studio. Maybe recording was a balm.

I never did find a need for J., nor for the interim bass player who had gone from a light collaborator to a running commentator on my musicianship. Somehow, there just wasn't room for either of them. In that way, the record felt protected to me. Like I didn't invite the vampires into the house, after which, it's hell to get them out. I'd already had enough run-ins with the drainage and wanted to keep something for myself, and I did.

The bass player left Boston later that year, but I would see him again. We would go on to know each other for many more years before we called it for good. But that's a different story. In this one, he left, I finished the album alone, and it was later mixed in that same magical studio by Paul Kolderie himself. Squire left, too. He went back to his home state of Maryland before he ended up in Los Angeles. One by one, the town was getting smaller, and I was still there.

And J.? After that night at the Middle East, I never saw her again. And not just in that chapter of the story. In my life. It was as though a forcefield kept us apart. In a town where you couldn't leave the house without seeing five people you knew, we became instant strangers.

But it wasn't over. Not quite. Sometimes you have to bury the body to make sure something is dead.

And we did.

Distortion

January 7, 2017, 9:48 PM Central Time

Hi Buick. I was surprised to see you pop up on Facebook. Figured I would say hi. After all this time, I wanted to say that I am sorry about being so controlling when you were in the band. I was definitely an asshole to you. I guess living literally twice my life since that point help me to see things with more perspective. Glad to see you are still making music. I only play with my kids these days.

* * *

In my season of making amends, I started to receive some. Not from any of the people who had done the serious damage but amends just the same. This person reached out about his behavior in a high school band; his, not mine. I had been recruited as a vocalist by another member when we were sixteen, and this guy, the drummer, had rejected all of my

ideas from the downbeat. A minor crime in the grand scheme of things, but it was good to receive the message just the same

That said, it's amazing who carries remorse about what in this life, and who does not. It's absolutely amazing. That's the word.

* * *

The first time I heard that I was being blacklisted in the scene, I was at a party. A woman who was a friend of a friend stood in the center of a circle and loudly told everyone that J. had announced that I was out. I was one room away and caught the gossip mid-sentence. Katie. Her name was Katie. She was spreading the Bad Word and delighting in her duty. Her face was in a wild smile. The listeners were intrigued, leaning in. *Why? What had happened?* And she told them what she knew. She had a real future ahead of her as the woman who would someday hate her son's female friends, I could already tell.

If you've never been present for a gossip session about yourself, let me tell you, it's electrifying. As in, it feels like parts of your system are short-circuiting. No grounding to be found.

This sort of thing started happening all over town. Second-hand shaming by way of women I knew through this-or-that person, one of whom, I worked with. Toward the end of my days in Boston, I was the assistant manager in a costume shop at a music conservatory. One of those jobs you end up with because you have a skill set that loosely applies, though your interests and culture do not. I am not, and have never been, a proper theater kid, but I've worked a few jobs that put me next to them.

This woman, Laura, had been hired after me, shortly after she moved to the area from somewhere nearby, like New Hampshire. Because Boston is the smallest town in the world, she started dating one of the guys in J.'s bandmate's other band, the emo outfit. Thus, while she was not a musician herself, she was privy to the scene gossip and social fluctuations.

I had been otherwise insulated from the overlapping of my worlds until this union. I was in rough shape one day at work and mentioned to a co-worker that my now-ex-best friend was going after me in my scene. Laura, from across the room, looked at me, smirked, and said, "I saw her over the weekend. I think she's nice."

Nice. What a word. What a choice. What a moment.

J. was a woman in her mid-thirties, and so was Laura. When I think about that now, about being older than someone you don't like and making the choice to speak ill of them in a town the size of a Walgreens . . . it seems many things. Nice is not among them.

The news that J. and her partner no longer wished to know me ignited like lighter-fluid-assisted-kindling, a rather dramatic response to a friendship ending, but I suppose something has to be thrown on the fire if we want to keep it burning. I told almost no one. She told almost everyone. And I got to find out the fast-and-flaming way exactly what the community response would be. They'd side with the loud one. The one who had more connections. The one who held more cards. And I didn't fight back. I didn't do shit. I just let it burn. The Katies and Lauras of the world are a tough group to be up against, especially when you factor in the grim realization that they were just waiting for someone else to make it okay to dislike you out loud.

Nice. One wonders what they consider to be not nice. I still don't know.

The small town got smaller, and the number of people in my corner dwindled. Allies like Marc had long moved on to places where one might enjoy some anonymity and breathing room. Places that might actually qualify as cities. I didn't even have the support of my partner. He was mostly gone, but when he was there, he pled the fifth. He was a man of few conflicts if he could help it. No one was ever wrong in his eyes, a nice gig if you can get it. I imagine being the youngest child, the only boy, the special one, and a person who was never abused or belittled might afford you such an outlook.

I wouldn't know anything about it.

Plus, he liked J.'s partner, a man whose music and notoriety were on the rise in a scene adjacent to his. He wanted him as an ally, and he got to have him as such. He got to write off what was happening between J. and myself—what had *been* happening for years—as trivial nonsense between women, something to look past. He and his community had already looked past one of their own backing me up against a wall at a wedding, telling me all the reasons he would never want to end up with me, have sex with me. I'd spoken up back then, and the lot of them had made it smaller than it was. The one time anyone mentioned the rampant substance overuse or abuse was when a man behaved inappropriately. It was otherwise invisible and inadmissible as a problem.

It seemed that the men had other, more important things to connect about. It wasn't afforded to me. I was a woman. It was something I was reminded of almost every hour of my life, especially in this new, exhilarating season of realizing I was socially disposable.

And then, right in the middle of it all, I got the email.

I received an email from J., a mode of communication that had previously been used between us for sharing lyrics and other such creative artifacts. We were not email pals.

The email, among other things, confirmed an ending. She had chosen not to know me anymore, and she had constructed an itemized list of reasons why. It would have been a fascinating read, were it not for the nausea and head-spinning it brought on. I was given a list of my unacceptable behaviors over the course of our seven-year friendship, one that included gossip, negativity, being unsupportive to the people in my life, and a bad overall attitude. She needed more positivity, she explained.

It would be years before I would understand that the reason the list of behaviors made no sense to me, was because they were not mine. They were hers. Note for note, the things she claimed I had said and done, had been said and done by her. But in the moment—in that season, and the many that would follow—I felt shame on a level that I had not known before, not in that specific way. I was being told that I was unacceptable, unknowable. And by someone I had let see my childhood home, who had stood next to me in my wedding, who had pumped me for every detail of my inner thoughts and feelings for the better part of a decade. And it had all been rated. Bad. No good. Throw it back. Worse, there was absolutely no way of knowing what she had said to other people. And she had certainly said something.

The ending of the email, and the true ending of our connection in this life, was one sentence.

And no matter how much time passes, I'll never get over the fact that it was added.

"I guess I'll just be one more person to leave you, to let you down, like your real father."

What, in the catalog of human experiences, might possess someone to say such a thing, I sincerely hope I never know.

Nice. Laura had called her *nice*. Well, best of luck to you both, Laura.

This sentence exists in a file of one-liners I've received in my life that were intended to maim. There are other ways to say, "Hey, you know what? This isn't working for me. Let's move on." There are other ways to let people go. I've lived long enough to have ended all kinds of relationships, romantic, professional, personal, and otherwise. You don't have to draw blood, and you don't have to weaponize vulnerabilities—yours or theirs. And if you do, you'd better be under the age of twenty-three. You'd better be young enough that you can later chalk it up to a yet-unformed brain. If you're thirty-four and you're trying to find a vein, there's something else going on with you.

And that something, I'm here to report, after years of thinking on it, is one word:

Cruelty.

That's the defining line.

It's the difference between hitting someone with your car because you didn't see them in the street and swerving to hit them. It's intentional. It's knowing. It's acute.

Listen, no one is getting out of this life without injuring someone and being injured. We're a messy lot, imperfect in our comings and goings. We scrape against each other with our insensitivities large and small, our judgments and fears. We do. Hence the process of assessing the damage every once in a while. Hence the amends we feel moved to make via Facebook Messenger. But there's a wide berth between inadvertent injury and intentional injury, and I'm afraid of people who trade in the latter. I've known a few, and I'm flat-out afraid of them.

I wish I'd had that distinction and clarity at that moment, but I did not. I unspooled, quietly and out of view. It wasn't what was said. Who cared about some absent father figure you never lived with, never called "Dad," and never knew well enough to lose? Okay, I did, a little. But not enough for that to be the entry point of the knife. It was that she knew I'd experienced that slow-motion abandonment from him, and she'd used it. That was the part that chilled my organs and almost froze them to death. I'd shown her everything. And she'd used it.

* * *

When I first started making amends in recovery, it was important for me to keep my own motivation in mind. It wasn't about forgiveness, or hoping the other person would like me again. I didn't even like some of them if I'm being completely honest. It wasn't about that. It was about saying, "I see what I did, and in this current chapter, I'm doing my level best not to repeat it." It wasn't about

reconciliation, and it wasn't about friendship. It was and is about ownership.

I have come to learn that the Cruelty Set don't think anything belongs to them. Don't hold your breath waiting for those amends, loved ones. They'll let you die out there.

* * *

There was no good place to be anymore. Once you've become the main character in an insular scene, you either ride it out, or you leave. I did a little of both. Because I was married, and because I didn't have much money, movement was slow. But the ex-communication meant that playing music in Boston now came with a built-in level of discomfort that had never been there before, even when I was in the insipid project with J.

I felt embarrassed all the time. I started moving through the town differently. I would walk instead of taking the train. I'd drive. However I could minimize my chances of running into other people, I would. I went to work and behaved like I was fine, like I was unmarred, unfazed. I had learned that showing my injuries only invited more. Those little girls who had seemed so hard when we were kids had grown into adults, and they hadn't softened one bit. Any sign of weakness was an opening in Boston. You felt badly about yourself? Here was another reason to feel worse. You were afraid? Run. You felt unloved, disliked? You were. Something happened to you? Walk it off.

There was one notable exception to this line of thinking, as far as I could tell, and that was physical illness of any kind. They would honor cancer or a horrific accident. Someone I'd gone to high school with had thrown himself in front of the Red Line and lived. That mattered. Of course, no one talked about the underlying mental illness or suffering that might have preceded the jump, though. It was all about the body. Even still, if someone from those days falls ill, I get a text or an email, and then it's all hands on deck. But emotional injury was and is a non-category. Too bad. Pull yourself together. Deal with it in the dark.

I'm wired for something else, but I have pretended otherwise at times. It's a survival thing.

I allowed myself to become consumed by my jobs. I started working more than ninety hours a week. The kids at the conservatory didn't know I had been cast out. They didn't mind me being around all the time. The work was distracting and numbing. I could forget who I'd been, what had happened, and also that I was now in a marriage that didn't observe injury of any kind. How retro. How Catholic.

I let myself wander away from that marriage, mentally and emotionally. I let myself wander away from who I had known myself to be. I didn't understand how to do it, the people thing. Not in Boston, and maybe not anywhere. It was always the shunning and the being backed up against hard surfaces. The groups of people looking right through you while it happened. The silence. The pretend. The bullshit. If you asked questions, you were out. If you set boundaries, you were out. If you showed your tits on own your tour poster, you were out. If you did anything outside of the ever-changing set of guidelines, you were out. And so, really, why bother? Might as well just completely unplug from the wall and be separate. And I was. I looked great, and I was deeply undone. Not one person cared.

When I told my husband I was leaving, moving to Brooklyn, it was a statement. Not a question. Not, "Hey, what do you think about moving to the New York area?" No. It was merely a statement to inform him of my changing whereabouts. We moved in August of that year, and he left for tour a few days after we got there. Fine. I was alone again, but I was alone in a new place where I had no history. And so, my loneliness lifted. I was starved for anonymity, for new streets, stores, and sidewalks. I would be new. I would be unknown. I would be free. If you're going to be alone, you might as well be free.

A Retraction

July 1, 2018, 1:19 PM Central Time

Sorry to miss you guys again!

We got to MA on Friday for vacation.

("Vacation" and "MA" should not

go together)

Oh no problem!

Yeah, MA is like **The Shining**

for me and I try to never go there.

But I hope you have a good time!

* * *

The people in my life who also left Massachusetts are the only ones who make jokes about the place. He and I had both been gone for a million combined years. His parents still lived where they did when he and I dated during my one year at Belmont High, but he had since relocated to the New York area. And unlike so many people I'd known when we were kids, we had stayed in touch. We weren't reunited by social media. I could be honest with him that Boston was akin to a Stephen King novel for me. He could take it.

Other people were another story entirely.

* * *

I was in Brooklyn for four years before I moved to Nashville. And while New York wasn't the absolute clean slate I'd hoped for, it was a better life. My partner's entire band followed us there, so his world stayed intact. I remained outside of it and created my own.

When I came to Nashville, I came alone. And for a while, Boston was far away. Over a thousand miles away on the map, but fewer miles away online. And now, some of those Massachusetts people live here. The world of music is connected for better or worse. But the way I feel within it has changed. It took a lot of work in my recovery, and the luxury of distance, but I see things differently now.

* * *

The shame followed me for years. It lived underneath my skin, in my posture, in everything I said and did. Some of it was older than the experience with J., and with Boston. Some of it had been there all my life; it was inherited, taught, and then fortified. Shame was an early dialect, passed on by my parental figures and other relatives.

My very existence had been a mistake, and they told me that. Then they couldn't keep it together, and she left. He became something other, far away, an uncle of sorts. He showed up with beer and they played songs in the back yard until dark. He didn't look at me, speak to me, or seem to wonder about me. The abuse was all my young life, from before my memories began up to the time she left and took us to Boston when I was nine. They knew, and yet it happened. They knew, and I was left alone with the old man, the babysitter built-in to the family. They knew, and yet I was blamed for naming it. More shame. Plus, the drinking, the guns, the lying. Lying was the language of the land. Taught, like a subject. How to tell anything but the truth. How to fit in, how to look the same. Different school every year, blend in. Nothing about you works or fits. *Blend in.*

I never blended. I still don't.

By the time I got back to Boston at age sixteen, I was merely getting by. And it makes so much sense to me now, that I would have allowed anyone—absolutely anyone—into my world; that belonging could have had any price tag attached to it, and I would have paid. Happily. The idea that I was fundamentally unlovable on a cellular level was already in there. But what happened in Boston proved it to be true. Out here in the real world, not just in the context of my sick and suffering family systems. And it happened in large and small ways. It wasn't any one person's fault or doing—until it was—but it was a pattern of rejection and aggression that ultimately led to my ex-communication from a scene I had once loved and longed to be a part of. It was crushing. It was also dangerous.

When Marc died in the summer of 2020, there was something I couldn't get my mind around, much less my heart or my words. I couldn't find the piece of it that went past the profound loss of this man I had loved for decades. I couldn't see the splinter that had gone in too deeply to be pulled out.

More than a year later, I wrote a song called "A Retraction" and said some things within it that I hadn't seen coming. It surprised me at first. The song was essentially pulling previous sentiments from rotation, claiming their value to be null due to a new awareness of self. A new clarity. All the *I love you*-related transcripts needed to be pulled from the shelves of a certain history. For, I had not known myself well enough to have dispersed them in the first place. And while the whole of the statement was startling, I knew instantly that it was about Boston. About that marriage, those friendships, those ties. The sentiments were moot; I had been compromised.

The next song that came, about two months later, was about Marc directly. About how, in all of the bullshit, amid the now absurd ocean of love and solidarity with unworthy ghosts, I had maybe never told Marc how much I liked and cared for him. I spent time with the truth that it had been easy to love and know him, that I hoped he knew anyway; I hoped it had been a respite for him, as it had been for me. I was having a hard time talking about him in the past tense, so that went into the song. I could still close my own eyes and see his, smiling and blue in the Cambridge sun, looking right at me; that went in, too. Intermittently, and often, I wept during that writing process. I called the song "Fail." The failure was in being late, and in not knowing he had been at the edge.

And as I sat in that dark blue grief of missing him, I knew. I knew it was time to look at everything else. There had been a curtain up for years between me and that place, and with the exception of artfully dodging the cast members, I hadn't had the strength to look. I wrote the rest of the record in a handful of weeks. It gushed out of me like it had been waiting there behind a barrier.

Once the music existed, I was able to see the piece of Marc's death that was not solely about the loss, the part that woke me up. It was so simple.

What happened in Boston could have killed me, and I believe it nearly did. The months that followed the ex-communication were the only high-risk months of my life. I have spent incredible amounts of energy and time trying to protect myself from outside things; it has informed every part of how I live. But in that season, I came off the frame. I didn't care if I lived or died. I didn't think I was allowed to. That was the culmination of the old and new shame. And it almost got me.

I understood Marc's death. That was the piece.

The forgetting, as strange as it was, had been a relief. It had provided a frost on the glass between me and that history. I never lost any time before or after it, but Boston had been mostly deleted by the part of my system that was trying to stay alive. Marc's death wiped the glass. If I wanted to grieve him with an open heart and a clear mind—and I did—I would have to look through the lens. I was still alive.

I wear a necklace that says, "Still Alive." I had it custom-made after Friendship Commanders released our 2020 EP, *HOLD ON TO YOURSELF*. It's part of a line from the song "The Enemy I Know." The song, and the EP in general, are about being an adult survivor of childhood abuse. It was the first body of work in which I addressed my status as a survivor of things I understood to be damaging. Physical abuses. Violations of my personal autonomy. Violence. It wasn't until Marc died that I was able to name the other things that could have taken me. That awareness was arresting.

* * *

The residual shame was around the shape of what had happened, and it rippled out for a long time. Was I defective for not being able to do this female best friend thing that had been pitched to me as the one and only true way to be? Nobody around me talked about female friendships ending, and certainly not in this scorched earth kind of way. It was loneliness on top of loneliness, and it didn't do much in the way of convincing me that showing up as myself was acceptable. Having needs, an identity, and standards for myself seemed to be at odds with the whole arrangement. The last part of it was trust. Trusting other women. Trusting myself. Trusting any further dynamics as safe—or at the very least, not toxic.

I wish I could report a perfect score here. I wish I could say that all future friendships with women went swimmingly, that we all vacation in

Napa together and go to brunch, or whatever it is we're all seeing on social media. That's not what happened.

Unsurprisingly, the remaining female friendships I had from the Boston days were colored by what happened there to varying degrees. Though I would go on to know some of them for quite a while after the fact, I was still trying to be the most loving, agreeable, giving person on earth. The fear of being unknowable was driving all of my choices, and I went on to maintain dynamics with women that centered and elevated men, that minimized my musicianship and artistry, and that saw me attempting to get along with everyone and everything. Lonely friendships for me.

As the years have gone on and my ways of relating have changed, many of those relationships have fallen away. And it's okay. Most of the time, it's okay. I changed, so we changed. It's simple math; it's a harder truth.

Sometimes all you have is the past, and sometimes that past isn't so hot.

Those were difficult losses for me in different ways, but nothing will ever match what happened with J. There can only be one of those in this life, one that cuts that deeply.

When I got to the end of the Lost Women inventory, I saw my tendencies quite clearly. I had spent time around some people with whom I had few shared values or interests; people I might never have met, had it not been for a job, a boyfriend, or a mutual acquaintance. They were in my path, in my immediate vicinity, and connected to other people, places, and things. I didn't know that I could choose. I didn't know that I could say, "No thanks," and see myself out. I really didn't. I thought that any person who showed interest in me was mine to know. Make it work. Sort it out. Find a way. My rejections had started so young, I believed that being accepted hinged on accepting anything, anyone.

In not choosing, I had merely allowed myself to be chosen. The inventory was a two-and-a-half-year tour through my own passivity. And within that passivity, there had been dishonesty. It was not intentional, or anything I could have seen at the time, but by trying to fit myself to what other people expected of me, I had shown up dishonestly. This wasn't true across the board, but it was true often enough that I could also see the pattern of endings once I *did* arrive as myself. It wasn't what they had bargained for, and I had played a role.

When I close my eyes and try to see past the last part, past the mocking, the confusion, and the shame, did I even like J. when I met her? Honestly? Sure, some. I might have even loved her at times. But not enough for it to have become what it did, or to have burned the whole town to the ground. That was a bit much.

The other part that emerged once my personal shame started to dissipate, allowing me to become an adult in the story, was the question: what was everyone else doing?

No part of my friendship with J. could have looked anything close to normal to the people around us. In fact, upon asking my brother what he remembered of it, he confirmed that it had seemed wildly out of balance. But he was younger than me and assumed I knew what I was doing at the time. Fair enough. But what about the people in J.'s generation? They had all watched a much older woman drag another woman around in identical clothing, chastise her in public, and then enact a social destruction campaign against her. And no one said, "Hey, what's going on here?"

No one?

Not one person asked me, "Are you okay?" Worse, some of them would lazily give me news updates about J. and Co. sightings as the years marched on. Like I might possibly have been interested. The mind reels.

Today, when I get those messages about standing up for other people—because I do, I have stood up for people in this life—what I see is that no one stood up for *me*. And some days, that feels like a bigger betrayal than what J. did. Apologists live in a cold room in my heart, I have to say. They're all just looking out for themselves, and for the status quo.

There was social capital at stake, after all. And the threat of being different, which—if we've learned anything here, friends—was not celebrated. But it doesn't make them people I can know, and that's a sad pill to swallow, one that a younger version of myself would have rejected. I ingest it now. I matter, too. And I mattered then. I'm not on this earth to stand up for everyone else and be flattened in the process. Not anymore.

I spent decades scouring myself for compassion for others. I could see the contexts. I understood the systems that contributed to why most people did what they did. I got it. What I didn't have, and what took the loss of a dear friend to find, was compassion for myself. Not only had I lived through some things, but I believed I deserved them. I believed that my childhood abuses made me so odd, so ill-fitting, that the ways other people responded to me were inevitable. That they'd had no choice but to treat me poorly. For that, I have tremendous compassion today. For the Boston scene at that time, I have less. And I feel fine about that. May they all do their own adult work. Godspeed.

* * *

In early 2022, I got a message on Instagram from someone who had been at the Philadelphia show on the now quite memorable tour, the one for which we'd printed the tits-out posters. She found me on my socials to ask if the 33 Slade records were streaming anywhere. They weren't. I'd released *Harmonies for One* on my own once I moved away from Boston, but that fog of shame was still with me at the time, and I played the release small. I told her where she could buy physical copies and thanked her for reaching out.

She came back with a surprising amount of praise for both the show she'd seen and my voice in general. We ended up messaging back and forth about that time, about what had happened. I kept it vague, but I gave her the broad strokes.

After that exchange, it struck me as rather surprising that I'd kept going musically after Boston, but I had. I'd moved to New York, started a new life, started making solo albums, and eventually came here and started Friendship Commanders. It wasn't as tidy as all that, but I'd kept going.

I scanned myself for a reason why.

What I found, was the tiniest flame of "*fuck you*." That was what had been there all along, ever-lit. It wasn't confidence, it wasn't self-love, and it wasn't even the will to live. It was just a flicker of "*fuck you*," and it had been enough. Now it's a larger fire that I tend and protect, but even when I didn't, it existed like a pilot light somewhere within me.

And it never went out.

Move

September 2, 2021, 12:27 PM Central Time

Happy birthday Buick. How is your brother Bowie? I was really confused when I saw that you said you were raised in Miami? Buick I'm confused. You and your brother Bowie with your mother were in Belmont Massachusetts for most of your upbringing. Buick then went on to work at the tobacco store in Harvard Square Cambridge Mass. I'm just extremely confused.

* * *

There's nothing quite like being told about yourself by someone who never knew you. By someone you went to some middle school with, but who now feels qualified to send you bizarre messages on social media—and who seems more interested in your sibling than you. Aside from the many factual liberties taken in the message (my birthday is February 23rd; my brother's first name is spelled BOEY;

I lived in Belmont, Massachusetts for a grand total of seven years throughout my youth and young adulthood, and those years were broken up into three time periods), the tone is wild. And never mind the last bit when he starts speaking about me in the third person, *to me*. That detail is better left unexamined.

In case it needs to be restated: I am from Miami. I always will be. But Massachusetts has a way of claiming things, and people, as it turns out. I have received versions of this communication over the years. Buick from Boston. Buick who worked here, or went there, etc. I have no concrete explanation for it, but I have a theory. The first part of that theory is that some people decide that what they see is simply what is, period. The second part is a profound lack of curiosity. If you never ask, you might never understand. And before you know it, you're messaging a stranger.

* * *

It wasn't all bad.

I lived at 18 Verdun Street in Dorchester, Massachusetts for the last seven years that I was there. When I think of that time and place, I think of that apartment. It was the second floor of a three-level house, all levels of which had the same layout. There was a foyer as soon as you entered, and identical sets of rooms on each side of the apartment. Three and three. Each room was connected to the next by a door, with the exception of the bathroom, which was in the center back. It had wood floors and a beautiful built-in hutch in what I called the dining room even though we never dined in there. We carved pumpkins in there once a year. I made all kinds of things in that room, from hand-screened punk rock underwear to the first printouts of the script for a rock opera I wrote and produced. Once, a bat flew into the apartment and spent the night in there, sleeping upside-down, hanging by its toes from the picture rail. Like a tiny Dracula. I do believe it was one of the most exciting events of my beloved cat Amos's long life.

Initially, I moved into that space with Mel when we were at MassArt, but I stayed on after he moved out and lived there with practically everyone I ever knew. It was a base, a true home base. I'd never had one as a kid, but I gave myself one as a young adult, and I lived there until I left Boston for good. There were some less-than-great moments there, of course, but it was a haven for me; I'm grateful to have had it.

I played my first shows in Boston. I became a songwriter and guitarist in Boston. I attended my first Alateen meetings in Boston. I learned to drive in Boston. I got my degree in Boston. That's all with me today. A lot of things are.

I walked. The walk from Boston to Cambridge across the Mass Ave. bridge was one of my favorites, no matter the season. I passed the original Cheers bar, which everyone in Massachusetts likes to tell tourists is nothing like the one on TV. I passed the old Necco factory, its pastel confections harkening back to an earlier time. I passed about three-hundred colleges and universi—kidding. But it truly is the land of higher education. What I'm now surrounded by in churches, I was once surrounded by in schools. I liked it. I liked knowing that people were up to something inside each of them. I was, too.

I probably walked every street of Boston and Cambridge, no exaggeration. The one-way streets of Cambridge, some of which were paved with bricks or cobblestones, were favorites, especially when you'd catch some out-of-towner sailing down them the wrong way. Cambridge is a tall order for visitors.

I worked. I had some jobs that paid absolutely nothing, but which were fun and educational. I worked at a consignment bridal shop on Sundays when I was in high school; I spent the day with a woman in her twenties, just the two of us. We put the dresses on over our clothes when no one was in there, took Polaroids of each other, and went next door for coffee and blueberry cake donuts when the shop was dead. I inspected the architecture of those sacred garments when I could and took mental notes about their structures. I remember those Sundays with a fondness so strong, it's almost unbelievable to me. But I'll take that feeling where I can get it.

I did work at the old tobacco store in Harvard Square, Leavitt & Peirce, when I was in college. It was a hilarious job for someone who had never smoked anything, but it paid the bills and kept me in coffee from Toscanini's next store. Working there was like being in a lost Kevin Smith film, a motley lot of young people being managed by a rigid-but-likable powerlifter whose family owned the business. L&P was and is directly across the street from Harvard and is the oldest business currently open in Harvard Square, having opened in 1883. It's so old that the interiors of the space are historically protected. If they shuttered tomorrow and a Forever 21 were to open in its place, it would be a Forever 21 with a black and white checkered floor, a cigar and chess parlor lofted space, and glass cases that once held meerschaum pipes and other olde tyme fare. My favorite experiences there were when the store was closed, and I was tasked with setting up the front windows for the holiday season. I'd put on music, pull everything out of the window bays, clean them, and then make festive magic out of chess games, razors, and fake snow while the real snow fell on the other side of the glass. People would stop and look at what I was doing, and we'd smile and wave.

It was fine for a time; I wouldn't pin my whole identity on it.

I danced. I danced all the time when I lived in Boston, multiple times a week for a couple of years toward the end. I didn't drink, I didn't smoke, but I would dance until they turned the lights on at 2 AM and told everyone to go home. For a while, I liked seeing others and being seen, and that was real; it wasn't performed. I felt like myself when I danced, and I liked everyone more when they danced. It was honest. Some things had been honest.

I made art. I found my way into the oasis that was Roger Mulford's art room in Belmont High when I was sixteen, not as a student, but as a wandering teen with a free period. A friend was in one of his classes, and I'd go in and hang out with her until my next class. Mulf didn't care, nor seem to abide by any of the school's rules about having kids in your class who weren't supposed to be there. He'd mock-scold me and call me to his desk at the front of the room, directing me to take "giant steps." Once I was there, he would hand me a brochure for Massachusetts College of Art. I'd laugh and thank him, but I had no idea what motivated him to do that. Other times, he would walk past my friend's table where I was posted up, and wordlessly drop a brochure in front of me.

I enrolled at MassArt with no formal visual art background under my belt. While I was there, I made everything from fabric, to garments, to large-scale color photo collections featuring me as Barbie in 1963. Somehow, Mulf knew.

At MassArt, I was fortunate to study under a bold sculptor named Taylor Davis who was then an adjunct professor. She helped me understand why being able to present and defend my work in any medium was essential. She taught me about isolating the "why" of it all, and clearly stating it. I'm not sure I've ever received better teaching from anyone, and I still use the education almost daily. I graduated with honors at the age of twenty-four.

I knew joy. Some of my favorite memories of my brother are from that time, whatever the backdrop may have been. Between crises, we were and are a funny set of siblings, as different as we are alike. In some circles, we were so inextricably linked that someone coined the names Boick and Buey; in others, no one knew we were related. Whenever someone would ask us how we knew each other, Bo would say, "We share a mother." (Pretty good, Bo. Pretty good.)

We gave each other shit, we played in bands, we lived together, we fought. Best time ever.

I had family. I went to Arthur's house all the time, but the Passover seders were standout occasions. I was vegan and could eat little on the table other than the charoset, but I'd have a salad and participate in the rites just the same. Sometimes Jared and I would get the giggles in response to the seriousness, just as Bo and I had done as kids during Catholic mass with our grandmother, but Arthur would keep the whole thing on track. I loved being there. One of the last times I attended before I moved, Arthur's longtime girlfriend told me she dated Arthur for more than a year before she realized I was not one of his actual children. Arthur spoke about me the same way he spoke about his sons. For all of my reclamation of self I've felt called to do in this life, for all of the un-choosing, it was moving to hear that. I had been claimed by someone safe at least once. I had been loved. Known.

To be known.

I had friends. In the young years before the Miami sabbatical, and before I moved back for the last time, I shared some moments with other girls that still shine. Walking from Belmont to Watertown with Leigh Wiley when we were eleven. Going to the Arsenal Mall to look at Claddagh rings. I had no idea what they were, but I loved the trip. Coming up with dance routines in Shara Abdoo's basement. Wearing Theresa Puleo's white strapless semi-formal dress on stage at the middle school talent show to sing "Where Do Broken Hearts Go" by Whitney Houston. Unreal, ridiculous times. Fun times.

I also had love. This story isn't about that, but some of it was real.

It wasn't all bad. In fact, some of it was all-time great. And that was buried, too, underneath the strain. Underneath the wreckage. Writing the album as the memories came back was akin to going underwater and looking at a lost city, holding my breath so I could see as much as possible before coming back up. It wasn't possible to stay down there for long, and it wasn't possible not to return. Once I could see it again, I wanted to know more.

It wasn't all bad. But it was bad enough that the other memories—the good ones—were colored blue by the difficult ones. Water-stained and warped, waiting to be pulled apart from one another. And now I've seen them.

When I was there, it was my whole world. Even though I was from elsewhere, the Boston story grew up around me like English Ivy. Pretty to the uninformed eye but destructive if it goes too far. I let it climb too far. At some point—and it's hard to pinpoint exactly when that was—I stopped wondering about other places, about leaving. And then one day, leaving was the only thing that made sense. I didn't even have a chance to miss anything.

Now I think about Massachusetts like it's a member of my family. Familiar, formative, with a shared history. But I don't speak to everyone in my family.

The Verdun Street apartment had been great. 33 Slade Street had been great. The nachos at Cantina la Mexicana in Union Square had been the best of my life (in desperate moments, I've Googled whether or not they can be shipped to Nashville; friends, the prospects are not good). I made a few precious, valued relationships that continue to this day. And I made steps toward becoming who I am. That all counts. The good stories count. They're just not the only ones I tell today. Today, I tell the whole thing. What a relief.

I also make deliberate, informed choices these days. I choose who I spend time with, what I wear, how my hair looks, how much power I put behind my voice, and what music I do and do not make. And the people who offer commentary on any of that get moved to an outer ring. I don't need that anymore, and I don't give it space.

I still occasionally have folks slide up next to me who want to drill me about this or that, who try to establish unearned intimacy; people I can tell dislike me but want to be around me anyway;

people who want to take on parts of my identity or compete with me. I can feel it now. And I know better. Pretending those tendencies in other people don't exist is a one-way ticket back to hell. They do exist, and I have choices about how I respond to them.

I don't spend a lot of time applying gendered tropes to which people I should be friends with anymore. If I'm on a text thread about the *John Wick* films with two dudes, that's fine. If I have a running text conversation with a guy in town in which we exclusively talk about the weird, short-run Gibsons we both like and which pick-ups we might put in them, that's fine. Anyone who takes issue with any of it needs to be doing their own work on gender and what we expect of women. I wish them the best of luck, too; it's a ride.

I don't answer questions about how my brother is doing, nor any other adult man who has a phone number. If you're not asking me how I'm doing, I'm not answering. I can't believe that has to be stated.

I stay away from the people who tell me *about* me, and who weren't paying attention in the first place.

I do my best to honor Marc and what I learned from losing him by keeping an eye on who I am in the lives of my friends, not just who they are to me. I hope that they feel known. I matter and they matter. I am one half of each relationship: no more, no less. Those days are over.

I go where it's warm, toward the people and things that make me want to live. I know the alternative, and it's not worth it.

Last, because I believe the past serves as a guide to the present, I don't use the term "best friend" to describe any of my current relationships. It's not for me. There are a few people I'm close to, but we don't need the titles. And I don't need to maintain any systems I inherited. I'm designing new ones.

* * *

Someone recently asked me if I always knew I would tell this story. To which, I said, "I didn't think I would ever tell this story. I didn't know it was a story until Marc died."

I just thought it was my life.

Dissonance

July 7, 2021, 6:51 PM Central Time

Hey! Just realized that Converge has a show in LA on 12/10 and we'll probably need to rehearse for it first. Any chance we could move the dates from 12/3-8 to 12/1-6? Also, I'd like to mix Dec 16-18. Does that work?

* * *

Jerry wanted to work with Kurt years before we actually did. The first time he brought it up to me, in 2017, I said no. I'd never met Kurt and had nothing against him personally, but the very idea of going to Massachusetts to work with a person—a man—from there was a No. Deep in my stomach, it was a Hell No. And then the campaigning followed. We'd be in the van and suddenly I'd be listening to Code Orange or High on Fire, the Ballou records. It went on like that for a while.

We'd already been recording ourselves for some time and were in the market for an engineer to be part of the equation. We didn't want to be performing and keeping track of the mics and all that. Something always manages to be wrong with one mic and you don't find out about it until you've done basics for five songs. It's the stuff of meltdowns and needless finger-pointing. An engineer would be nice, we agreed. He wanted Kurt; I wanted anyone in any other state.

After months of not giving in, I gave Jerry an option: if Kurt would get on the phone with us and I could feel him out, I'd consider it. I can usually tell if someone is a monster in fairly short order these days, a skill set that's been honed over years of unfortunate dynamics. Jerry agreed to ask Kurt. And then we waited.

The call happened weeks later, during an FC tour. We were in a hotel room in Portland, Oregon when Kurt called. After Jerry spoke

with him for a short time, he handed the phone to me. I had one primary question, and I led with it.

"How do you feel about women?"

To date, he's the only man who has answered with a modicum of honesty.

* * *

We worked with Kurt for three years before we ever met him in person. He came on as a mix engineer for the *HOLD ON TO YOURSELF* EP, which we made at the end of 2019. Then he mixed all of our pandemic-era singles, which we later released as a vinyl compilation called *RELEASE THE REST*. We didn't actually work with him right away after that fateful call. We worked with Steve Albini first, and that collaboration was a terrific experience. By the time we started to work with Ballou, there was less pressure on the whole arrangement. We loved his mixes of our work. They were easy to love.

Jerry still wanted to work with him in person, and eventually, I did, too. Kurt and I had become email friends during the pandemic. He talked me into building my first guitar pedal and sent me a care package of his proprietary PCBs to get me started. I liked him well enough, and working with him long distance had eased me into the idea of going up there. We started to sketch out a plan. By the time he sent that email about the December dates, I only had one song partially written, "A Retraction." We had scheduled the dates early for logistical reasons, but the record wasn't written yet. I wasn't worried. I'd already written several records in a couple of short months. It can work.

I didn't know it would be a concept record at first. I wrote a couple of songs, they happened to both be about Boston stories and then it built from there. By autumn, the fact that we were heading to Massachusetts to make a record about Massachusetts felt like a prophecy fulfilled. Things were snapping into narrative and conceptual place on an hourly basis. When the record was about seventy-five percent written, I suggested a name. *MASS*. Every definition worked. Assembly, groups of people, the religious rites, massive quantity, Massachusetts.

Done.

We had a tour booked for the two weeks leading right up to our allotted studio time. It was going to be a tight turnaround, but we stared it down. I finished writing the last song the day before we left for the tour. It was called "Move." On our days off on that run, we rented rehearsal space time and practiced the album. It was all brand-new material, but it was also a shift for us. The music itself was different. Some of it was heavier, some of it was songy-er. But we believed in it, and I trusted the music that had come through. When things assemble into a body of work that quickly, I tend to trust it, even if it's unknown in more ways than one.

By the time we arrived at GodCity in Salem the night before we were scheduled to start tracking, we were exhausted. We both like being tired. We perform better. We're looser, more natural. Kurt opened the door and couldn't have been more likable. Like a metal science teacher. Perfect.

We had six days scheduled to track nine songs. Everything but the vocals. I like to record my own vocals. Not always, but a lot of the time. Albini tracked the vocals for the *BILL* album—to tape, at that—but most of the time, I like to have the room to explore vocal options, layers, harmonies, and emotional performances without an audience. This practice was originally borne out of wanting to distance myself from abusive recording engineers, but now it's just about liking my own process. We had time built in between tracking the music and Kurt's mixing window. I would come back to Nashville, sing, and then the tracks would go to him for mixing. Salem was all about the instrumental performances.

After about a day of working together, it seemed unbelievable that Kurt and I had never met. We had so many people in common, it was almost absurd. Still, he'd never known Marc, and I couldn't remember ever seeing Kurt in any room I'd ever been in. There was no prior history between us. And I had no prior history with Salem as a place. FC played Salem maybe twice when we first started touring, and both of those experiences were benign. It didn't feel like Boston out there. It felt like its own thing, and all of that was a boon.

During that week of tracking, we worked eight-hour days, stayed in a small-third floor apartment we rented on Airbnb, and shut everything else out. We did tell Kurt that the record was about my time up there, and he was an adult about it. He'd already heard the news that life wasn't perfect for everyone on earth, and therefore wasn't surprised by an album about it. How refreshing. The three of us co-produced the instrumental tracks in between long talks about being kids in Boston, every recording engineer we had in common, vegan food, etc. If left to our own devices, Kurt and I could have easily started a podcast that week. Luckily, Jerry was there to facilitate forward movement. I do think the talking helped, though. I think it helped to make it feel like a scalable mountain. It introduced ease. Kurt is oddly disarming.

The tracking went as smoothly as it has ever gone for us. GodCity is small, so drums were set up and recorded with me in the room playing scratch guitars. We then struck the kit, tracked Jerry on bass, and then set up my rigs for tracking the guitars. It was three and a half days of guitars.

I have learned that I prefer to record with engineers who make their own work, and who take creative risks. In the cases of Albini and Ballou, it has helped me to trust them as both engineers and co-producers. They know what it's like. In theory, that should make them more empathetic on the other side of the glass. True to my theory, Kurt was great to track guitars with.

He gave responsible, helpful feedback, he followed my lead about my tones and preferred gear, and he helped me not dwell on what I believed to be my pitfalls.

It was, as I have come to call records made in this chapter of my life, a cruelty-free recording process. What a thing. And Salem did a fine job of being a conflict-free zone. Someplace new. In Massachusetts. Where I could make new memories. And we did.

The morning after we finished tracking, we walked to the end of the street we had stayed on all week and looked at the bright, cold water. We took a photo to mark the spot. We'd done it. All I had left to do was sing it. On the drive home, I jotted down parts of something else I was hearing. Something spoken. To be determined, I thought.

The initial timeframe allotted for the vocals was under six days. In past projects, that would have been no problem Too much time, even. I sang the *BILL* album (twelve songs) in something like six hours. The vocals for *HOLD ON TO YOURSELF* (five songs) had been cut in a day. But I got home to Nashville, and almost immediately, I knew it wasn't happening. For starters, I was a little sick. With the touring and traveling to the Northeast to make an album, that wasn't a surprise. But I was also emotionally fatigued. I would get two passes of a song down and need to lie down. The album was written and instrumentally recorded, but I had greatly underestimated the singing.

Additionally, the songs varied in what they asked of me. It wouldn't be all power-singing for this body of work. Some of what I heard in my head was softer. "High Sun" and "Fail" both required something else of me at parts. And then there were the feelings. The feelings were closing my throat.

I emailed Kurt and said that the timeframe wouldn't work. My voice was giving me trouble, I was a little sick, and I didn't want to cram. We moved the mix dates to the end of the month.

At first, the vocals beat the shit out of me. They did. I sang, I cried. I walked around the block. I talked to Marc. I trusted myself, and then I took that trust back and distrusted myself. I sang leads in batches, I listened later. It was all over the place. And then I got methodical. Nine songs. Forever performances. Story of a foundational chapter in my life.

Get it together, Buick.

Start at the beginning, and sing.

I taped a bright yellow piece of paper to the front of the mic with one word printed on it.

Care.

We knew the album's sequence when we cut the instrumental tracks, so I went back and started at the beginning. The beginning was "Blue," a song written to remind myself—and anyone else who needed to hear it—that we are not the people around us. We are not the road behind us. We belong to ourselves. Get up to that mic and sing it. Done.

Second song, "Fail." You loved Marc. Tell him. Tell him here. Maybe he can hear you, maybe he can't. But *you* can hear you, and his death changed your life. His friendship made it immeasurably better. Say it now. Done.

Next up, "High Sun." She laughed. They watched. You know something about that. Your parents watched, too, when you were a kid. You know about being scapegoated to keep the status quo. You've known since you were small. But you're not small now. Say it with your whole body. Done.

"Vampire" is the one you heard in your head when you got to the part of the story when she tried to unzip your skin and wear it as her own. When she took the music you loved, your style, your courage, and wore it all as a costume. Sing it the way she would have shamed you for doing so back then. Whole-ass voice. Be big. Done.

Everyone who called you rigid, brittle, and judgmental when you flagged your own assault, when you were rightly afraid of unsafe people when they pretended no one had an addiction or an affliction. You put it into "Still Life" like a time capsule. Sing it. Done.

When you finally let the words fall out of your mouth that you had lived in constant fear that you were unlovable when you were there, it became "We Were Here," and you cried for a full day after writing it. So true, it knocked you down. You're up to bat, kid. Done.

It's okay that you used to downplay what had happened in your young life. They trained you to do that, to be grateful for the abuse and abandonment, to abandon yourself in the process. It lives in "Distortion" now. Go get it. Done.

That first song, the one about how you couldn't have known what you were saying to anyone else back then because you didn't even know yourself. It's called "A Retraction," and it gave you this record. Sing. Done.

And "Move," the bookend to "Blue," reminding you and the sky above that it's okay to leave. Nothing about you is required to stay behind, to make it work, or to be the glue. Get your shit and go. And while you're at it, sing this last song. For you at sixteen, for you at twenty-seven. You did it. You're done.

But was I done? The singing was done. Jerry had some synth ideas that stuck, and some handclaps that were later walked back. The odds, the ends. Those last stages of a record that is probably done but which you just can't quite let go of. But I had one more thing.

My van notes had assembled into a kind of thesis. Not a poem exactly, not a song, but a piece. I called it "Dissonance." I had never recorded a spoken piece before, and as it turns out, it's not the easiest thing to do. Every single ambient sound in your world is suddenly audible. The set-up used for tracking rock vocals is not the one you use for spoken audio, I learned. I set up an SM7 in my office and got under a blanket, and for the first and only time, read my piece into the mic. Jerry heard it for the first time when it was already tracked.

And then it was done. The tracks were sent back up to Kurt the day after Christmas and he mixed it in two days.

Truly done.

* * *

In the weeks and months after we finished the record, I started to share some of my recovered memories in a series of flash non-fiction pieces called *Massachusetts Memories*. Some were on the more benign end of things, but others were not; some dipped into J.'s controlling behavior toward me, her correcting my words and actions in public, and my fear of being autonomous. And as I shared those pieces, an interesting thing happened. Boston people just loved them. But not for what I was actually showing; for what they saw of themselves in the writing, in the locations, in the narratives. They had each managed to find sunny things to attach themselves to. As bizarre and disappointing as that initially was for me, it served as great validation. That was what had happened back in the day, too. Same thing, different year. I had been right. The sky *is* always blue in Massachusetts.

I could sense myself feeling betrayed by those responses, the younger self inside me still wanting to be seen and known by those people. But I don't need them to see and know me today. I see and know myself, and that's the real headline. It happened. And I'm allowed to tell the story whether or not anyone I used to know gets it. I don't have to assign that much power to them anymore. Plus, they're allowed their own lens, even if it features an ever-blue sky. I get it; I really do.

Not all stories are happy stories. Not all stories illustrate exemplary behavior and nostalgic arcs about groups of people who each did their very best. I'm sorry, it just isn't so. Not all stories are tragedies, either. I believe, if we're willing to get honest with ourselves, and with each other, it is possible to find the grey in between. I believe the grey is where the real connection lives, the possibility for intimacy, the way to recovering. It has been for me. And I'm still doing it. This work will continue. I think I might be done telling the Boston story, but in doing this Big Dig (that one's for the true Massholes), I found other things. In time, I'll look at those, too. It takes care. It takes time. It takes courage.

In the meantime, in my current life in Nashville, I sometimes run into someone from the old Boston days. I understand that he played drums in some band of men or other. Nice enough guy. I have exactly zero memory of him. Nothing. I know his name and his old band's name, and nothing else comes up. I wave and say hello when we see each other in restaurants, but for all the Massachusetts memories I've recovered in recent years, the files on him remain empty. And I think that's fine.

I've remembered enough.

This is enough.

Acknowledgments

To Jerry: thank you for all of it; for loving me through this process of holding my breath until I could see the full picture; for never judging what I brought back; for bringing it into the sunlight with me. Thank you for trusting and knowing me.

To Kurt: thank you for meeting me where I was, for making it sound huge, for holding the space.

To Boey: thank you for your witness, your support, and your contributions to my life. I am so grateful we were thrown together as siblings in this life.

To Marc: thank you for leading me back, for reminding me that it didn't need to be so difficult, and for your easy friendship. I hope that you felt known.

To Arthur: thank you for welcoming me, for treating me like a person, for your steady love and respect. I will miss you all of my days.

To Taylor Davis and Roger Mulford: thank you for knowing who and what I was before I did, for modeling artistic integrity, and for taking a chance on a weirdo kid when she needed it. Mulf, you were a king among men.

To Jared: thank you for modeling true friendship, for the laughs, and for the letters when I was away. I still have them.

To Leigh Ruocco: thank you for being kind when we were kids, and for being kind now. You stand out as a consistent bright spot.

To Amos: thank you for raising me through all of this mayhem. I might not have survived it without you.

To Julie: thank you for being a safe and loving constant, and for helping me through the inventory of Lost Women.

To Levi: thank you for then and now. We're still here.

To everyone who let me use their quotes for the essay intros: thank you. They helped a great deal.

To you, listener: thank you for being here.

To twenty-seven: good for you. Fuck those people; keep going.

Twenty-seven.

Old Language	New Language
dependence	autonomy
co-existence	intimacy
best-friendship	control
community	scapegoating
respect	gaslighting
familiar	identity
resilience	grief
love	regret
commitment	agency
definition	duality

About the Author

Photo by Anna Haas

Buick Audra is a Grammy-award-winning musician, songwriter, and writer living in Nashville, TN. In addition to her solo work, she is also a member of the melodic heavy duo, Friendship Commanders. She has published several essays, and one previous essay collection, *Conversations with My Other Voice: Essays*.

www.ingramcontent.com/pod-product-compliance
Lightning Source LLC
Chambersburg PA
CBHW051307120626

46547CB00015B/2134